DIABETIC COOKBOOK AND MEAL PLAN FOR THE NEWLY DIAGNOSED

Sophie Gosens

© Copyright 2021 - All rights reserved.

The content contained within this book may not be reproduced, duplicated or transmitted without direct written permission from the author or the publisher.

Under no circumstances will any blame or legal responsibility be held against the publisher, or author, for any damages, reparation, or monetary loss due to the information contained within this book. Either directly or indirectly.

Legal Notice:

This book is copyright protected. This book is only for personal use. You cannot amend, distribute, sell, use, quote or paraphrase any part, or the content within this book, without the consent of the author or publisher.

Disclaimer Notice:

Please note the information contained within this document is for educational and entertainment purposes only. All effort has been executed to present accurate, up to date, and reliable, complete information. No warranties of any kind are declared or implied. Readers acknowledge that the author is not engaging in the rendering of legal, financial, medical or professional advice. The content within this book has been derived from various sources. Please consult a licensed professional before attempting any techniques outlined in this book.

By reading this document, the reader agrees that under no circumstances is the author responsible for any losses, direct or indirect, which are incurred as a result of the use of information contained within this document, including, but not limited to, errors, omissions, or inaccuracies.

Table Of Contents

INTRODUCTION 8
   What Exactly Does a Diabetic Diet Entail? 8

CHAPTER 1: WHAT IS DIABETES? 10
   Types of Diabetes 11
   What Can Be Done to Avoid and Manage Diabetes? 12
   5 Diabetes Prevention Tips to Help You Stay in Check 12
   When Do You Schedule an Appointment With Your Physician? 13

CHAPTER 2: A HEALTHIER LIFESTYLE 14
   What Does a Diabetes-Friendly Diet Look Like? 15
   10 Tips for a Diabetes-Friendly Diet 15

CHAPTER 3: NUTRITION: WHAT TO EAT, WHAT TO AVOID 18
   Low Starch Food 19
   Non-Starchy Vegetables 19
   Fatty Fish 20
   Dairy 20
   Beans and Pulses 20
   Fruits 21

CHAPTER 4: 21-DAY MEAL PLAN 22

CHAPTER 5: BREAKFAST RECIPES 24
1. Apple Topped French Toast 25
2. Cafe Mocha Smoothies 25
3. Cauliflower Breakfast Hash 25
4. Cheese Spinach Waffles 25
5. Cinnamon Apple Granola 26
6. Coconut Breakfast Porridge 26
7. Cottage Cheese Pancakes 27
8. Ham & Jicama Hash 27
9. Hot Maple Porridge 27
10. Jicama Hash Browns 28
11. Blueberry Breakfast Cake 28
12. Whole-grain Pancakes 28
13. Buckwheat Grouts Breakfast Bowl 29
14. Peach Muesli Bake 29
15. Steel-Cut Oatmeal Bowl with Fruit and Nuts 30
16. Whole-Grain Dutch Baby Pancake 30
17. Mushroom, Zucchini, and Onion Frittata 30
18. Spinach and Cheese Quiche 31
19. Spicy Jalapeno Popper Deviled Eggs 31
20. Lovely Porridge 32

CHAPTER 6: LUNCH RECIPES 34
20. Asparagus with Scallops 35
21. Butter Cod with Asparagus 35
22. Creamy Cod Fillet with Quinoa and Asparagus 35
23. Asparagus and Scallop Skillet With Lemony 36
24. Butter-Lemon Grilled Cod on Asparagus 36
25. Lemon Parsley White Fish Fillets 37
26. Cilantro Lime Shrimp 37
27. Cajun Catfish 38
28. Tomato Tuna Melts 38
29. Peppercorn-Crusted Baked Salmon 38
30. Roasted Salmon with Honey-Mustard Sauce 39
31. Ginger-Glazed Salmon and Broccoli 39
32. Roasted Salmon with Salsa Verde 39
33. Whole Veggie-Stuffed Trout 40
34. Ginger-Garlic Cod Cooked in Paper 40
35. Roasted Halibut with Red Peppers, Green Beans, and Onions 41
36. Blackened Tilapia with Mango Salsa 41
37. Scallops and Asparagus Skillet 42
38. Baked Oysters 42
39. Tropical Shrimp Cocktail 43
40. Pork Chop Diane 43
41. Chipotle Chili Pork Chops 44
42. Orange-Marinated Pork Tenderloin 44
43. Homestyle Herb Meatballs 44
44. Lime-Parsley Lamb Cutlets 45
45. Mediterranean Steak Sandwiches 45
46. Roasted Beef with Peppercorn Sauce 45
47. Coffee-and-Herb-Marinated Steak 46
48. Traditional Beef Stroganoff 46
49. Pork Chops with Grape Sauce 47
50. Roasted Pork & Apples 47
51. Pork with Cranberry Relish 47
52. Sesame Pork with Mustard Sauce 48
53. Steak with Mushroom Sauce 48
54. Steak with Tomato & Herbs 49
55. Beef & Asparagus 49
56. Italian Beef 49
57. Barbecue Beef Brisket 50
58. Lamb with Broccoli & Carrots 50
59. Beef Chili 51

CHAPTER 7: DINNER RECIPES 52
60. Wholesome Broccoli Pork Chops 53
61. Lemony Dijon Meat Loaf 53
62. Italian Pork Chops 53
63. Tomato Steak Kebabs 54
64. Pork Mushroom Stew 54
65. Beef Steaks with Green Asparagus 55
66. Garlic Chicken Balls 55
67. Mu Shu Lunch Pork 55
68. Bacon & Chicken Patties 56
69. Autumn Pork Chops with Red Cabbage and Apples . 56
70. Creole Braised Sirloin 56
71. Crispy Chicken Wings 57
72. Herb Butter Lamb Chops 57
73. Rosemary Lemon Lamb Chops 58
74. Herb Garlic Lamb Chops 58

#	Recipe	Page
75.	Delicious Lamb Chops	58
76.	Pork Tenderloin with Bell Peppers	59
77.	Pork Tenderloin with Bacon & Veggies	59
78.	Pork Rolls	59
79.	Pork Sausage Casserole	60
80.	Lemon Chili Salmon	60
81.	Tuna Burgers	61
82.	Breaded Cod	61
83.	Salmon Patties	61
84.	Spicy Catfish	62
85.	Vinegar Halibut	62
86.	Lemony Salmon	62
87.	Spiced Tilapia	63
88.	Buttered Salmon	63
89.	Crispy Fish Sticks in Air Fryer	63
90.	Honey-Glazed Salmon	64
91.	Basil-Parmesan Crusted Salmon	64
92.	Halibut Ceviche with Cilantro	64
93.	Ginger Cod Chard Bake	65
94.	Peppery Halibut Fillet with Beans	65
95.	Fruity Cod with Salsa	66
96.	Broiled Cod Fillets with Garlic Mango Salsa	66
97.	Butter Cod with Lemony Asparagus	67
98.	Cod Fillet Quinoa Asparagus Bowl	67
99.	Tuna Onion Broccoli Casserole	67

CHAPTER 8: SIDE DISH RECIPES 70

#	Recipe	Page
100.	Coffee-Steamed Carrots	71
101.	Rosemary Potatoes	71
102.	Wonderful Steamed Artichoke	71
103.	Mashed Pumpkin	71
104.	Parmesan-Topped Acorn Squash	72
105.	Low Fat Roasties	72
106.	Roasted Parsnips	72
107.	Lower Carb Hummus	72
108.	Parmesan Cauliflower Mash	73
109.	Steamed Asparagus	73
110.	Squash Medley	73
111.	Eggplant Curry	74
112.	Lentil and Eggplant Stew	74
113.	Tofu Curry	74
114.	Lentil and Chickpea Curry	74
115.	Kidney Bean Stew	74
116.	Fried Tofu Hotpot	75
117.	Chili Sin Carne	75
118.	Carrot Hummus	75
119.	Garlic Sautéed Spinach	75

CHAPTER 9: SALAD RECIPES 76

#	Recipe	Page
120.	Tomato, Cucumber, and Avocado Salad	77
121.	Green Salad with Blackberries Vinaigrette	77
122.	Summer Salad with Honey Dressing	77
123.	Cucumber and Kidney Bean Salad	78
124.	Spinach and Chicken Salad	78
125.	Kale, Cantaloupe, and Chicken Salad	78
126.	Cobb Salad	79
127.	Sofrito Steak and Veg Salad	79
128.	Zucchini Salad with Ranch Dip	80
129.	Spinach, Pear, and Walnut Salad	80
130.	Grain, Seafood, and Fruit Salad	80
131.	Asian Noodle Salad	81
132.	Cabbage Slaw Salad	81
133.	Three Bean and Basil Salad	82
134.	Rainbow Black Bean Salad	82
135.	Warm Barley and Squash Salad	82
136.	Winter Chicken and Citrus Salad	83
137.	Blueberry and Chicken Salad	83
138.	Buffalo Chicken Salads	83
139.	Wild Rice Salad with Cranberries and Almonds	84

CHAPTER 10: SOUPS AND STEWS RECIPES 86

#	Recipe	Page
140.	Authentic Gazpacho	87
141.	Tomato Kale Soup	87
142.	Zucchini Soup with Roasted Chickpeas	87
143.	Thai Shrimp Soup	88
144.	Lime Chicken Tortilla Soup	88
145.	Split Pea Soup with Carrots	89
146.	Moroccan Eggplant Stew	89
147.	Cheeseburger Soup	90
148.	Taco Soup	90
149.	Lentil Vegetable Soup	91
150.	Quick Clam Chowder	91
151.	Beef Barley Soup	91
152.	Creamy Chicken Soup	92
153.	Broccoli and Chicken Soup	92
154.	Guinness Beef Stew with Cauliflower Mash	93

CHAPTER 11: SNACK RECIPES 94

#	Recipe	Page
155.	Mortadella & Bacon Balls	95
156.	Crispy Baked Cheese Puffs	95
157.	Raspberry Almond Tart	95
158.	Oatmeal Butterscotch Cookies	96
159.	Quail Eggs & Prosciutto Wraps	96
160.	Pumpkin Spiced Almonds	96
161.	Cheese Crisp Crackers	96
162.	Tortilla Chips	97
163.	Hot & Spicy Mixed Nuts	97
164.	Mozzarella Sticks	97
165.	Buffalo Bites	98
166.	Plum & Pistachio Snack	98
167.	Avocado and Tempeh Bacon Wraps	98
168.	Cinnamon Apple Chips	99
169.	Tofu & Chia Seed Pudding	99

CHAPTER 12: DESSERT RECIPES 100

#	Recipe	Page
170.	Ketogenic Lava Cake	101
171.	Keto Donuts	101
172.	Coconut Milk Pear Shake	101
173.	Cocoa Mousse	102
174.	Coconut Ice Cream	102
175.	Fruit Pizza	102

176.	Choco Peppermint Cake	103
177.	Roasted Mango	103
178.	Roasted Plums	103
179.	Figs with Honey & Yogurt	103
180.	Flourless Chocolate Cake	103
181.	Waffles	104
182.	Pumpkin & Banana Ice Cream	104
183.	Brulee Oranges	105
184.	Frozen Lemon & Blueberry	105
185.	Peanut Butter Choco Chip Cookies	105
186.	Watermelon Sherbet	105
187.	Strawberry & Mango Ice Cream	106
188.	Ice Cream Brownie Cake	106
189.	Air Fried Sugar-Free Chocolate Soufflé	106
190.	Easy Air Fryer Brownies	107
191.	Air Fryer Apple Fritter	107
192.	Grain-free Molten Lava Cakes (Air Fryer)	107
193.	Lemon Custard	108
194.	Slow Cooker Peaches	108
195.	Tiramisu Shots	109
196.	Keto Vanilla Mug Cake	109
197.	Chia Pudding	109
198.	Chocolate Mousse	109
199.	Chocolate Ice Cream	110

CHAPTER 13: OTHER RECIPES 112

200.	Italian Eggplant Stew	113
201.	Indian Potatoes	113
202.	Broccoli and Tomatoes Air Fried Stew	113
203.	Collard Greens and Bacon	114
204.	Sesame Mustard Greens	114
205.	Radish Hash	114
206.	Swiss Chard Salad	114
207.	Spanish Greens	115
208.	Rutabaga and Cherry Tomatoes Mix	115
209.	Garlic Tomatoes	116

CONCLUSION 118

INDEX OF RECIPES 120

Introduction

A diabetes diagnosis can be frightening particularly when it is first discovered. Most of the fear has come from the unknown, as well as accounts of complications that can result from long periods of uncontrolled blood sugar. People with uncontrolled diabetes are more likely to develop complications such as cardiac disease, stroke, vision loss, depression, kidney failure, and other issues. This, however, does not have to be your story.

It's important to realize that you can completely regulate your blood sugar levels and avoid falling victim to any of the frightening statistics you've read. And it's probably a lot simpler than you think. The aim is to keep blood sugar under control, as this will avoid more diabetes-related health issues. In fact, once you start following the eating and lifestyle routines outlined in this book, you'll likely notice that you're feeling better than you have in years and that your blood sugar levels are regular and stable. While some people may need medication, the good news is that many people with diabetes can control their condition by making simple lifestyle changes. This involves losing weight, exercising regularly, and eating a balanced diet if you are overweight.

Prediabetes affects over 86 million people in the United States, about one-third of those over 18 and half of those over 65, and the majority of them are unaware of it. Prediabetes is portrayed as having glucose levels that are essentially higher than normal not yet sufficiently high to be analyzed as diabetes. Prediabetes expands the danger of type 2 diabetes, coronary illness, and stroke. As per the US Places for Infectious prevention and Avoidance, up to 30% of overweight people with prediabetes experience type 2 diabetes within five years of being analyzed. It isn't required for you to be one of them.

While not all with prediabetes will experience type 2 diabetes, those who do are at a higher-than-normal risk. So speak to the doctor about assessing your own risk and having a quick blood test to check for diabetes. Find out what precautions you can take right now to prevent or postpone the onset of type 2 diabetes and other medical problems, if possible.

If you have prediabetes, you will lower the chances of contracting more severe problems by improving your diet and losing weight. Eating healthier entails eating a range of healthy ingredients (e.g., lean proteins or protein supplements, fresh vegetables, high-fiber starches, and healthy fats), balancing the diets to ensure you receive all the nutrition you require, and keeping to minimal portion sizes. It also entails taking meals and snacks on a daily basis to prevent severe blood sugar swings during the day.

What Exactly Does a Diabetic Diet Entail?

A diabetic diet consists of three meals per day, at daily intervals. This allows you to make better use of the insulin that your body generates or that you get from a prescription. A certified dietitian may assist you in creating a diet that is tailored to your fitness needs, preferences, and lifestyle. He or she may also counsel you on ways to change your dietary behaviors, such as selecting portion sizes that are appropriate for your height and level of exercise.

CHAPTER 1:

What Is Diabetes?

Diabetes is perhaps the most pervasive sicknesses distressing the overall population in the US. As indicated by the Communities for Infectious prevention and Anticipation (CDC), 1.4 million new instances of diabetes are analyzed in non-industrial nations every year. Not only that, but the problem is worsened by the fact that an estimated 8.1 million people are unknowingly living with the disease. As a result, diabetes affects 9.4 percent of the general population in the United States.

Diabetes is classified into three types; however, most diabetes patients have type 2 diabetes, which can be avoided by carefully balancing medicine and eating habits.

Diabetes mellitus is a form of diabetes that affects people (DM). It is a condition caused by elevated blood glucose levels in the body. Insulin, which aids in the conversion of glucose in our bodies into energy, does not always produce enough insulin in diabetic patients. Subsequently, glucose can't enter our cells, bringing about diabetes. This disease is not curable, but if left untreated, it can lead to a variety of bodily complications in patients. Diabetes causes acute complications such as diabetic ketoacidosis and hyperosmolar hyperglycemic condition. Frequent urination, thirst and hunger, severe weakness or fatigue, unusual irritability, nausea, vomiting and abdominal pain, and unpleasant breath are all symptoms of diabetes. In addition, diabetes can cause a number of severe long-term complications in patients. Cardiovascular disease, chronic kidney disease, heart attack, foot ulcers, impaired nerves, and vision loss are among them.

Types of Diabetes

Type 1 diabetes (insufficient insulin production by the pancreas), Type 2 diabetes (insufficient insulin response by cells), and gestational diabetes are the three most common types of diabetes (pregnant women diabetes history developing high blood sugar levels).

What is Type 1 Diabetes, and how does it affect you?

Type 1 diabetes, the most feared of it all, is also known as "juvenile diabetes" because it affects both children and adults. In Type 1 diabetes, the patient's body quits creating insulin, which is expected to separate sugar in the body. The insusceptible arrangement of the patients is debilitated accordingly. When the body ceases making insulin, a Type 1 diabetes patient must take insulin every day to stay alive. The autoimmune response causes the loss of beta cells; the cause of this response is unclear. However, some theories suggest that genetic factors can play a role in Type 1 diabetes. A family member who has a similar condition could be a risk carrier.

Since there is no solution for Type 1 diabetes, patients should be treated with insulin shots controlled by infusion simply under the skin or through an insulin siphon. The patient must follow a strict diet and exercise routine for the rest of his or her life.

What is Type 2 Diabetes, and how does it affect you?

This is the most common form of diabetes currently in use. Type 2 diabetes is very common among today's youth and adults. The essence of our lifestyle and lack of physical activity is one of the key reasons for this. Obesity and a lack of exercise trigger the condition. People who have a family history of the diseases are more likely to develop Type 2 diabetes. Type 2 diabetes, which was once only present in people over the age of 35, is now also being found in children and teenagers. At least 90% of diabetic patients are considered to have Type 2 diabetes characteristics.

This is a non-insulin disorder, which means that the patient has elevated blood sugar, but is not expected to take insulin shots on a regular basis. Patients with Type 2 diabetes contain insulin, but it is insufficient to break down glucose. Type 2 diabetes can be avoided by observing one's weight, rehearsing regularly, and eating a sensible eating routine, and continuing with a sound lifestyle. This ought to be adequate to keep a consistent glucose level. If the patient is still unable to control the amount, the doctor will normally prescribe medicine. Type 2 diabetes symptoms differ from type 1 diabetes symptoms in that they are less apparent. However, it is important to avoid gaining too much weight or ceasing to exercise.

What is Gestational Diabetes, and how does it affect you?

This type of diabetes, which typically develops during or shortly after pregnancy, is more common in women than in men. In Gestational Diabetes, women experience diabetes and elevated blood sugar levels during pregnancy, in some cases. Gestational diabetes can occur in pregnant women who have never had high blood sugars or diabetes before.

After the child is born, the disease seems to have disappeared as well. In certain cases, the mothers are discovered to have acquired the signs and symptoms of Type 2 diabetes after the child is born. Pregnant women who have gestational diabetes are more likely to develop Type 2 diabetes later in life. Gestational diabetes signs are difficult to detect, increasing the risk of pre-eclampsia, depression, and cesarean delivery.

What Can Be Done to Avoid and Manage Diabetes?

Changing your diet and eating habits is one of the most effective ways to avoid or regulate diabetes. Diabetes has infiltrated our lives and is affecting the well-being of today's children and youth, and was once a disorder that only impacted adults over 35. Heftiness and an absence of actual work are the main sources of diabetes.

- Patients with Type 1 Diabetes should depend on insulin infusions, either infused or controlled through a siphon, to keep their glucose levels stable. A high-maintenance diet, normally recommended by a doctor, should also be strictly adhered to in order to mitigate the effects of Type 1 diabetes.
- Diabetes often attacks the heart by causing damage to the blood vessels, which can lead to a variety of Heart-Related Diseases and Strokes. At all times, the patient should maintain a permissible blood sugar level and refrain from smoking.
- Hypoglycemia is a disorder in which blood glucose levels are abnormally low. Diabetic patients with low blood glucose levels should seek medical advice and adhere to a strict diet schedule.
- Chronic kidney disease, heart stroke, foot ulcers, impaired nerves, and vision loss are some of the other diseases that can affect diabetic patients.

Diabetes prevention necessitates lifestyle management, which is the safest treatment for a diabetic patient.

5 Diabetes Prevention Tips to Help You Stay in Check

When it comes to type 2 diabetes, which is the most prevalent type, avoidance is crucial. In case you're at a raised danger of diabetes, for example, if you're overweight, have a family background of the illness, or have been determined to have prediabetes, it's especially imperative to focus on diabetes anticipation (otherwise called disabled fasting glucose). Diabetes avoidance can be pretty much as basic as eating more soundly, getting more included, and shedding a couple of pounds. It's never past where it is doable to begin anything new. Making a couple of simple lifestyle changes can assist you with forestalling genuine diabetes-related medical conditions later on, like nerve, kidney, and heart harm. Consider the American Diabetes Association's diabetes prevention advice.

1) Increase your physical activity: Daily physical activity has many advantages. Exercise will assist you in the following ways:
 • Lose weight
 • Lower your blood sugar
 • Improve your insulin sensitivity — which helps hold your blood sugar in a healthy range

High-impact movement and strength preparation have been appeared to help manage diabetes in examinations. A health program that joins both offers the best benefit.

2) Eat plenty of fiber: Fiber can help you:
 • Decrease your danger of diabetes by improving glucose control
 • Lower your danger of coronary illness
 • Advance weight reduction by causing you to feel full
 • Natural products, vegetables, beans, entire grains, and nuts are high in fiber.

3) Choose whole grains: It's unclear why, but whole grains can lower your diabetes risk and aid in blood sugar control. At least half of the grains should be whole grains. Whole grain breads, pastas, and cereals are among the ready-to-eat foods made from whole grains. Look for the word "whole" on the box and in the ingredient list's first few products.

4) Lose excess weight: If you're overweight, losing weight might be the key to preventing diabetes. Every pound you lose has the potential to boost your wellbeing and you may be shocked by how much. Participants in one major study who lost a small amount of weight — about 7% of their starting weight — and exercised regularly cut their risk of diabetes by nearly 60%.

5) Avoid fad diets and instead make the following healthy choices: Low-carb diets, glycemic index diets, and other fad diets can initially help you lose weight. However, the efficacy of these treatments in combating diabetes and their long-term consequences are unknown. Furthermore, by eliminating or severely restricting a specific food category, you might be depriving yourself of vital nutrients while also increasing your cravings for certain foods. Make variety and portion control a part of your healthy-eating strategy instead.

When Do You Schedule an Appointment With Your Physician?

In case you're 45 or more seasoned, or an overweight grown-up of all ages with at least one extra danger factors for diabetes, for example, a family background of diabetes, an individual history of prediabetes, or an idle way of life, the American Diabetes Affiliation suggests blood glucose screening.

Your doctor would most likely prescribe screening every three years after the age of 45. Consult your doctor about your diabetes prevention issues. The person will be thankful for your endeavors to keep away from diabetes and make extra suggestions depending on your clinical history or different components.

CHAPTER 2:

A Healthier Lifestyle

What Does a Diabetes-Friendly Diet Look Like?

People with diabetes often believe that they must become hyper-focused on eliminating sugar or carbohydrates, ignoring the nutritional consistency of their diet. Despite the fact that carbs have the best impact on glucose, the entire eating regimen assumes a part in general wellbeing weight reduction, and glucose control. Strictly reducing carbohydrates found in fruits and whole grains when consuming a high-fat, high-sodium diet will not result in good health.

Focusing on healthy foods, portion control of carbohydrates, and losing weight if you are overweight are the three most effective things you can do to handle type 2 diabetes nutritionally. Also, don't feel obligated to lose an unreasonably small amount of weight—even losing 5 to 7% of your body weight will help lower blood sugar and reduce the need for diabetic medications. While the exact serving sizes will differ depending on the person, here are some general guidelines for a healthy diet:

- Burn-through a wide scope of products of the soil, just as entire grains.
- Attempt to eat two to three servings of fish every week.
- Olive oil, canola oil, nuts and nut butters, peas, and avocado are all good sources of heart-healthy fats.
- Limit sodium intake to less than 2,300 milligrams per day.
- Reduce the intake of added sugars, which can be found in a variety of processed foods and sweetened beverages.

10 Tips for a Diabetes-Friendly Diet

Sugar isn't always delicious. Consider the case of excess sugar in your bloodstream, also known as "hyperglycemia" or "high blood sugar level." One of the states that leads to diabetes is hyperglycemia. Diabetes mellitus is a chronic condition marked by blood sugar fluctuations brought on by inherited or non-standard dietary habits, as well as a sedentary lifestyle. There are many forms of diabetes, and no two diabetics have the same complications. As a result, a diabetes diet that is "one-size-fits-all" is unthinkable for diabetics. Furthermore, this form of diet aids in the regulation of blood glucose (sugar), blood pressure, and cholesterol levels. Also, following a doctor's or nutritionist's diet plan decreases body weight and lowers the risk of diabetes complications such as heart attacks and strokes, as well as organ degenerative health disorders such as some types of cancers.

Here are ten suggestions to help a diabetic patient change his or her lifestyle:

Tip #1: Eat three meals and three snacks during the day: To avoid hunger pangs, divide your daily food intake into three main meals (breakfast, lunch, and dinner) and three healthy snacks in-between meals. Snack portions should not be equal to any of the three meals; rather, they should be smaller. A safe bedtime snack can help a diabetic patient resolve hypoglycemia in the middle of the night or early in the morning (low blood sugar level).

Tip #2: Eat more complex carbohydrates: Complex CHO (carbohydrates) is far superior to simple CHO (carbohydrates). Since simple CHO (sugar, honey, jaggery, cookies, chocolates, muffins, fruit juice, carbonated drinks, plain rice, maida, sabudana or tapioca, etc.) contains no fiber, it is quickly absorbed, resulting in a blood sugar spike. Wheat, fruits with skin and pulp, rice with vegetables, salads, any kind of vegetable, wheat bread, wheat noodles, wheat pasta, and so on are complex carbs with a high fiber content (i.e., digestion and absorption take longer than usual).

Tip #3: Cut back on added sugar: We love sugar in our foods, and it can be difficult to avoid or reduce sugar/sugar variants at first. As a result, functional sugar substitutes are a good place to start. Low-sugar or "0" sugar beverages, zero-calorie energy drinks, coconut water, pure milk, buttermilk, various forms of flavored tea and coffee without added refined/natural sugar, and cut fruits with skin are all balanced sugar alternatives.

Furthermore, low- or zero-calorie sweeteners (i.e., artificial sweeteners) help us maintain a healthy weight and blood glucose level. The majority of store-bought sweeteners can do more harm than good to our bodies. Stevia leaves, on the other hand, are a better sweetener to use. When it comes to diabetes care, there are only a few cases of "hypoglycemia" (hypo) in which sugary beverages can be used in moderation. It is important in this situation that you do not reduce your sugar consumption as part of your diabetes treatment. If you have persistent hypoglycemia (low blood sugar), talk to your doctor and diabetes care team about your diet plan.

Tip #4: Consume a sufficient amount of high-quality protein: The Indian diet is deficient in both quality and quantity of protein. If you are a non-vegetarian, it is recommended that you have a substantial amount of first-class protein in your diet, such as lean meat, eggs, chicken, fish, and so on. A vegetarian plate, on the other hand, must include protein from plant and dairy sources such as broccoli, paneer, low-fat cheese, various pulses and legumes, soybeans, mushrooms, tofu, and so on.

Tip #5: Easier blood flow is aided by healthier fat: In our bodies, fat produces steam. Vitamins and minerals are absorbed into our bodies by fat molecules, providing us with energy and immunity. Are you aware that various forms of fats have positive and negative effects on our health? Cooking oil (such as rice bran oil, sunflower oil, sesame oil, canola oil, soya oil, corn oil, olive oil), unsalted nuts, beans, avocados, and oily fish are all good sources of healthy fats. Saturated fats, on the other hand, raise the level of bad cholesterol in the blood, resulting in heart disease and arterial blockage. Red and processed meat, ghee, butter, 'vanaspati', mayonnaise, cookies, cakes, pies, and pastries are all examples of animal products and processed foods. A life-long fitness tip will be to reduce the use of oils in general when cooking and instead use steam or baked foods.

Tip #6: Make sure you get your regular dairy fix: Dairy items such as curd, cheese, milk, buttermilk, or home-made paneer are sufficient to fulfill your body's daily calcium requirements. A diabetic patient's average daily dairy product intake should be less than 500 ml.

Tip #7: Fiber has a magical effect on blood sugar: Fiber is important in diabetic diet control because it helps to keep blood sugar levels in check. A diabetic's average daily dietary fiber requirement from usual ingested food is 25-35 gm (excluding any supplements). Fresh and cooked vegetables, whole fruits with pulp, whole grains, and legumes are the best sources of dietary fiber. Thus, a diet consisting of vegetable or lightly cooked leafy vegetables at three main meals and whole fruits for snacks will provide sufficient fiber.

Tip #8: Snacks that are light and tasty are a good idea: We all enjoy delectable treats. However, one can always choose snacks that are not only tasty but also nutritious. Low-fat yogurts, unsalted nuts (almonds and walnuts), flax/pumpkin seeds, fruits and vegetables, sprout salads, makhana (lotus seeds) instead of fried crisps, potato or banana chips, cookies, and chocolates are only a few examples. Portion size is sacred, and we must exercise self-control. As a result, relative to your main meals, the snack portion should be small.

Tip #9: Drink responsibly: Because alcohol has a high calorific value, it's best to drink in moderation if you want to lose weight. As a result, limit your alcohol intake to no more than 1 ounce per week. Keep an eye on the desire to binge drink, and practice going a week without consuming alcohol. In case you take insulin, or other diabetes sedates reliably, quit drinking alcohol on an unfilled stomach since it can cause hypoglycemia. Instead, you can drink alcohol (in moderation) at any time before or after dinner.

Tip #10: The body is made up of water, so stay hydrated: Water is rarely thought of as a nutrient in our diets. Did you know that water makes up to 60% of the adult human body? All of our cells, muscles, and tissues are nourished by water. Our bodies lose water through a variety of processes, including involuntary functions like breathing sweating and digestion. Water can be consumed at any time of the day, but it is recommended that it be consumed before major meals. Additionally, there should be a time period between meals when drinking water should be resumed. As a result, it's important to rehydrate ourselves by drinking enough water, non-sugar drinks, and consuming foods that contain natural water or freshly squeezed juices with pulp (rather than packaged or refined juices), as this helps lower our body temperature and keeps other body functions running smoothly.

CHAPTER 3:

Nutrition: What to Eat, What to Avoid

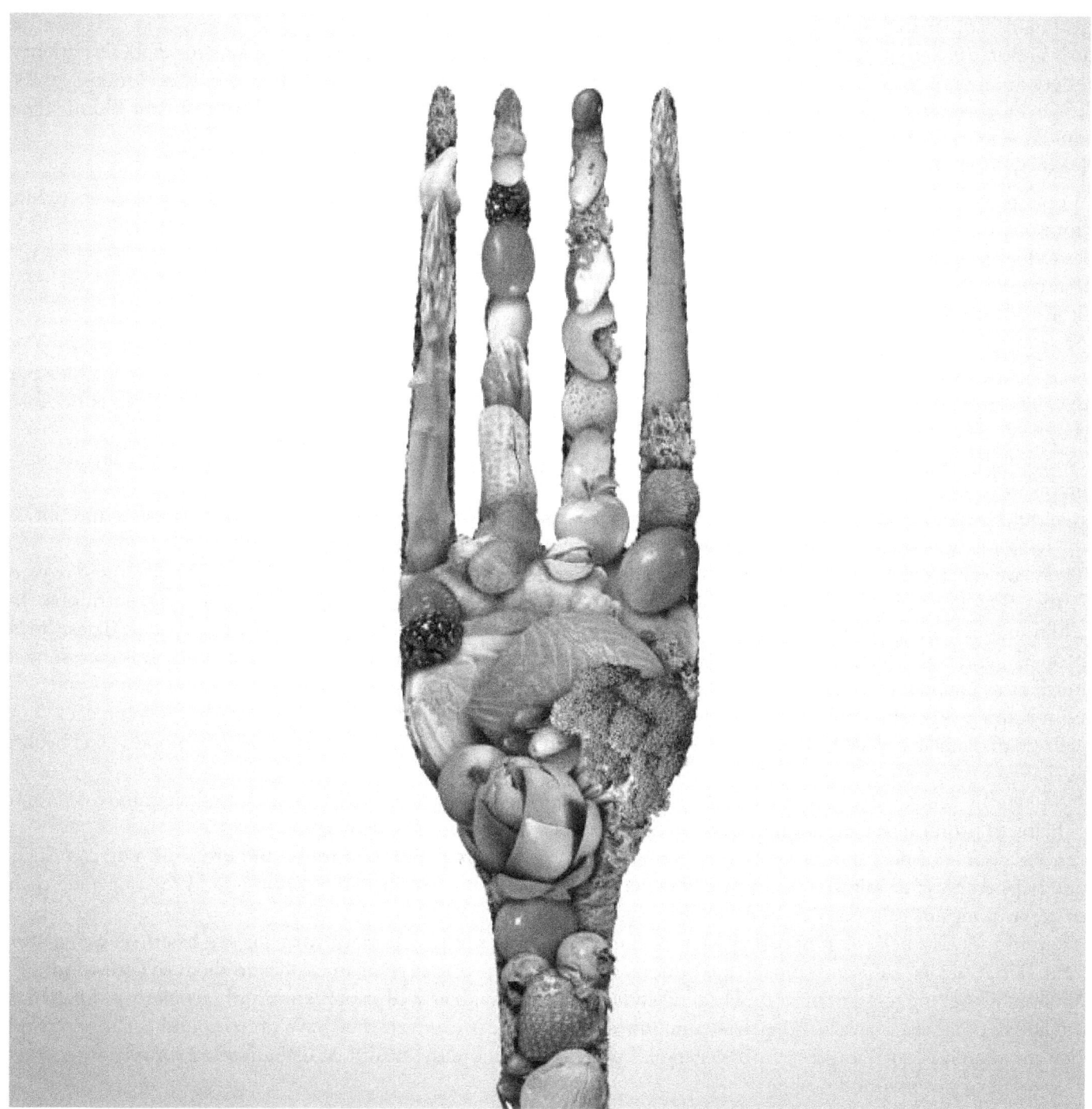

No matter what kind of diet you are attempting to follow, it is not correct to completely eliminate an entire food group. While with diabetes, there are certain food groups that you can try to minimize your intake of, such as starch and sugars but don't fall prey to the mistake of completely eliminating starch as your body needs carbs. Instead, you must choose wisely between the various food options in each category to ensure that you ingest the best and most suitable food type from each category and avoid the ones that will worsen your condition.

The goal of controlling your food with diabetes is eating food that will not increase your blood glucose levels higher than normal. At the same time, it must be food that fills you up and prevents you from being hungry; in addition, certain food categories can promote your health and provide you with nutritional elements that can help you fight off diabetes and protect you from its complications.

It is important to note that there is no one-size-fits-all when it comes to healthy eating plans for diabetic patients. There are lots of personal variations in the way our body responds to nutrition and different food intake styles; however, there are general rules that can be observed if you have diabetes and wish to control your blood sugar and keep its complications at bay.

Low Starch Food

Whole grains, for example, oatmeal, quinoa, and brown rice are preferred and healthier than white rice, white flour or processed grains, macaroni, etc.

Baked sweet potato provides a low-carb option in contrast to regular potato such as French fries. Other items that contain high carbs include white bread and white flour etc. Instead, opt for whole grain foods that have very little added sugar or not at all.

Non-Starchy Vegetables

One of the healthiest options if you're diabetic is to include a couple of servings of non-starchy vegetables per day. There is very little chance that you could go wrong with overeating non-starchy vegetables, that is because they have a very low calorific intake.

Non-starchy vegetables are vegetables that contain a small amount of carbohydrates. This is typically about 5 grams or less of carbohydrate per 100 g of serving.

It should be your goal that you have at least five portions of fruit and vegetables throughout your day, and out of those 5, it is best to have at least three of them that are non-starchy vegetables.

There are several reasons why non-starchy vegetables are very healthy options for diabetics. The foremost reason is that they are very low in carbs. Other reasons include how non-starchy vegetables are very nutritious. In addition, being vegetables, they are a critical source of dietary fiber. The dietary fiber will help you to digest food properly, and it also plays an important role in lowering your cholesterol levels. Overall, dietary fiber is an essential nutrient to include in your diet.

Non-starchy vegetables are a very powerful defense against the complications of diabetes. They help protect your cells from damage caused by diabetes and promote blood vessel health. They can also damage blood vessel health as diabetes progresses.

Non-starchy vegetables are also rich in vitamins and minerals such as vitamin A, vitamin C and vitamin K. Vitamin C helps to promote your immunity and protect your cells from oxidative damage.

A good source of non-starchy vegetables containing vitamin C are peppers, sprouts, and broccoli. You can easily add peppers to your salad or main dish. Steamed broccoli is also a very healthy option to add to your main dish or serve alongside salmon or to add to your veggie pan salad.

Vitamin E is also helpful in boosting your immune system; it is also important for your eye health as well as for your skin. Carrots, kale, and spinach are options rich in vitamin E that you can easily add them to your food.

Vitamin K is going to assist in wound healing and improving health as well as preventing atherosclerosis. Diabetics are at risk of atherosclerosis if they have uncontrolled diabetes. Moreover, they have poor wound healing so food rich in vitamin K such as green leafy vegetables will help promote the health of diabetics and prevent infections as a result of poor wound healing.

Below are Some Examples of Non-Starchy Vegetables

- Leafy vegetables: kale, lettuce, spinach, watercress, cabbage, Brussel sprouts.
- Root vegetables: carrot, turnip, radishes.

- Squashes: cucumber, squash, courgette, pumpkin.
- Stalk vegetables: asparagus, leeks, spring onions, celery.
- Others: broccoli, bean sprouts, mushroom, cauliflower, peppers, tomato.

As a diabetic, vegetables are your best friend. Fresh vegetables, when eaten raw or even when steamed, roasted or grilled, can be a very healthy low carb option. The same applies to frozen vegetables that are lightly steamed. Always opt for low sodium or unsalted canned vegetables. Canned vegetables with lots of added sodium are not a healthy option.

Also, it is counterproductive if you eat veggies that are cooked with lots of butter, cheese or a high-carb source. If you have hypertension or other complications of diabetes and metabolic syndrome, you need to limit your intake of sodium, including limiting pickles, etc.

Fatty Fish

Examples: Herring Salmon anchovies, mackerel, sardine.

Fatty fish is one of the most consistent diet recommendations when it comes to fending off diseases. Diabetes is no exception.

Since having diabetes poses a risk to your heart functions, it is important to take cardioprotective measures. Salmon contains Omega-3 fatty acids, which have a profound positive effect on your heart health. Taking care and promoting your heart health helps against the increased risk of heart disease and stroke that people with diabetes are faced with. In addition, studies have shown that several inflammatory markers had dropped when fatty fish was consumed 5 to 7 days per week for about 8 weeks. In addition to all that, it contains high-quality protein and is low in carbs, therefore, is perfect for maintaining normal blood glucose sugars after meals.

Dairy

Dairy food is an important food category and with a variety of choices available for you to pick from. Studies have shown that milk product consumption and total dairy products have been associated with a reduced risk of developing type 2 diabetes. It is also protective for those who have prediabetes. The mechanisms explaining this evidence are complicated but simply put, certain biomarker fatty acids found in dairy milk are associated with lowering the risk of developing diabetes type 2. The studies were conducted on each of the following items from the dairy group, including whole milk and yoghurt in addition to total dairy consumption.

Examples of dairy food include milk, yoghurt, cream, butter, and cheese. Unsweetened dairy products can be a very healthy choice for those who wish to follow a low-carb diet. There are numerous benefits for dairy foods as they are a good source of protein, calcium and vitamin B12. It is recommended by the National Osteoporosis Society that a daily intake of 700 mg of calcium is required for adults to maintain healthy bones as well as other functions that depend on calcium.

Vitamin B12 is an important source for the nervous system. Diabetics are at risk of complications of neuropathy that affects the peripheral nerves. Vitamin B12 helps protect against some of the complications of diabetes concerning the nerves. The protein in milk is also important for muscle repair and growth. The recommended daily intake of calcium can be achieved by just a pint of milk along with another source that includes food such as beans, fish with edible bones such as sardines and salmon and dark green vegetables, for example, kale and broccoli.

Opt for low-fat dairy, if you want to have high fat, or full-fat dairy, do so but in small proportions. The best choices are skimmed milk, low-fat yoghurt and low-fat or non-fat sour cream or cottage cheese. Some of the worst choices are whole milk, regular yoghurt, regular sour cream, cottage cheese and ice cream etc.

Beans and Pulses

Beans, pulses: lentils, peas, chickpeas, and runner beans are all examples of non-animal sources of protein that can be very beneficial for diabetics.

Soya Beans have been included in this group, and it has been supported with research indicating that the consumption of soya beans increases insulin sensitivity and reduces the risk of developing type 2 diabetes. In fact, certain countries in Asia have been using black soya beans to combat type 2 diabetes.

Adding beans to your salads is a good option for increasing your protein intake.

Fruits

Just like vegetables, fruits are one of the healthiest food groups that you can add to your diet. They are rich in nutrients, especially vitamin C, which helps to keep your cells healthy. In addition to the minerals, we also have fiber which helps digestion and it reduces cholesterol levels. Different fruits have a different combination of vitamins and minerals; for example, grapefruits can be rich in vitamin A as well as potassium; they can also be rich in vitamin K and manganese. A meta-analysis showed that groups of people who consumed a higher amount of fruits were at less risk of developing type 2 diabetes.

The American Diabetes Association recommends using fruits as desserts instead of sugary desserts, such as ice cream. While fruits have dense nutrients as well as fiber and antioxidants, it is important to remember that certain foods have a high glycemic index and can increase your blood sugar levels, therefore, it is important to be mindful about the types of fruits you eat and when.

Bananas and oranges are fruits that have a high glycemic index, while berries, for example, or less sugary.

Below are some examples of fruits that have a glycemic index of under 55:

- Grapefruit, Grapes, Kiwi, Apples, Avocados, Peaches, Plums Strawberries.

Fruit with medium glycemic index from 56 to 69:

- Pineapples, Papayas, Honeydew Melon.

Foods with a high glycemic index that is more than 70:

- Watermelon and Dates.
- Avoid processed foods such as apple sauce that have had their fiber removed. If you have a sweet tooth, fruits can be an optimum way to satisfy your desires without compromising your health. Since fruits are high in nutrients and low in fat and sodium, they are optimum if you have obesity or hypertension.
- One serving of fruit is a medium-sized fruit that is the size of the piece. Or a cup of smaller fruits such as berries. So, you should avoid it, but if you have processed fruits have only half a cup of processed fruits to fulfill the serving size.
- Apples. An apple is a versatile fruit that you can snack on raw or cook with some flavoring such as cinnamon or ginger to make a delicious dessert. You can also stuff your apples with some crushed nuts such as walnuts or pecans.

CHAPTER 4:

21-Day Meal Plan

Day	Breakfast	First Course	Second Course	Dessert
1	Apple Topped French Toast	Asparagus with Scallops	Wholesome Broccoli Pork Chops	Ketogenic Lava Cake
2	Café Mocha Smoothies	Butter Cod with Asparagus	Italian Pork Chops	Keto Donuts
3	Cheese Spinach Waffles	Cilantro Lime Shrimp	Tomato Steak Kebabs	Coconut Milk Pear Shake
4	Cottage Cheese Pancake	Asparagus and Scallop Skillet with Lemony	Garlic Chicken Balls	Fruit Pizza
5	Ham & Jicama Hash	Tomato Tuna Melts	Lemony Dijon Meat Loaf	Roasted Mango
6	Hot Maple Porridge	Peppercorn-Crusted Baked Salmon	Mu Shu Lunch Pork	Waffles
7	Jicama Hash Brown	Roasted Salmon with Honey-Mustard Sauce	Creole Braised Sirloin	Pumpkin and Banana Ice Cream
8	Whole-Grain Pancakes	Roasted Salmon with Honey-Mustard Sauce	Crispy Chicken Wings	Roasted Plum
9	Blueberry Breakfast Cake	Whole Veggie-Stuffed Trout	Rosemary Lemon Lamb Chops	Brulee Oranges
10	Peach Muesli Bake	Ginger-Garlic Cod Cooked in Paper	Delicious Lamb Chops	Frozen Lemon and Blueberry
11	Whole-Grain Dutch Baby Pancake	Roasted Halibut with Red Peppers, Green Beans	Pork Tenderloin with Bell Peppers	Easy Air Fry Brownies
12	Café Mocha Smoothies	Blackened Tilapia with Mango Salsa	Pork Rolls	Tiramisu Shots
13	Buckwheat Grouts Breakfast Bowl	Scallops and Asparagus Skillet	Pork Sausage Casserole	Peanut Butter Choco Chip Cookies
14	Cheese Spinach Waffles	Baked Oysters	Tuna Burgers	Watermelon Sherbet
15	Steel-Cut Oatmeal Bowl with Fruit and Nuts	Tropical Shrimp Cocktail	Lemon Chili Salmon	Keto Vanilla Mug Cake
16	Whole-Grain Dutch Baby Pancake	Pork Chop Diane	Spicy Catfish	Chia Pudding

17	Mushroom, Zucchini and Onion Frittata	Chipotle Chili Pork Chops	Salmon Patties	Lemon Custard
18	Spinach and Cheese Quiche	Orange-Marinated Pork Tenderloin	Vinegar Halibut	Ice Cream Brownie Cake
19	Spicy Jalapeno Popper Deviled Eggs	Lime-Parsley Lamb Cutlets	Honey-Glazed Salmon	Chocolate Mousse
20	Lovely Porridge	Roasted Beef with Peppercorn Sauce	Basil-Parmesan Crusted Salmon	Air Fried Sugar-Free Chocolate Soufflé
21	Cinnamon Apple Granola	Pork Chops with Grape Sauce	Ginger Cod Chard Bake	Chocolate Ice Cream

CHAPTER 5:

Breakfast Recipes

1. Apple Topped French Toast

Preparation time: 10 minutes
Cooking time: 10 minutes
Servings: 2
Ingredients:
- 1 apple, peel and slice thin
- 1 egg
- 1/4 cup skim milk
- 2 tbsp. margarine, divided

What you'll need from store cupboard:
- 4 slices Healthy Loaf Bread,
- 1 tbsp. Splenda brown sugar
- 1 tsp vanilla
- 1/4 tsp cinnamon

Directions:
1. Melt 1 tablespoon margarine in a large skillet over med-high heat. Add apples, Splenda, and cinnamon and cook, stirring frequently, until apples are tender.
2. In a shallow dish, whisk together egg milk, and vanilla.
3. Melt the remaining margarine in a separate skillet over med-high heat. Dip each slice of bread in the egg mixture and cook until golden brown on both sides.
4. Place two slices of French toast on plates, and top with apples. Serve immediately.

Nutrition:
- Calories 394 Total Carbs 27 g
- Net Carbs 22 g
- Protein 10 g
- Fat 23 g
- Sugar 19 g
- Fiber 5 g

2. Cafe Mocha Smoothies

Preparation time: 5 minutes
Cooking time: 0 minutes
Servings: 3
Ingredients:
- 1 avocado, remove pit and cut in half
- 1 1/2 cup almond milk, unsweetened
- 1/2 cup canned coconut milk
- What you'll need from store cupboard:
- 3 tbsp. Splenda
- 3 tbsp. unsweetened cocoa powder
- 2 tsp instant coffee
- 1 tsp vanilla

Directions:
1. Place everything but the avocado in the blender. Process until smooth.
2. Add the avocado and blend until smooth and no chunks remain.
3. Pour into glasses and serve.

Nutrition:
- Calories 109
- Total Carbs 15 g
- Protein 6 g
- Fat 1 g
- Sugar 13 g
- Fiber 0 g

3. Cauliflower Breakfast Hash

Preparation time: 10 minutes
Cooking time: 20 minutes
Servings: 2
Ingredients:
- 4 cups cauliflower, grated
- 1 cup mushrooms, diced
- 3/4 cup onion, diced
- 3 slices bacon
- 1/4 cup sharp cheddar cheese, grated

Directions:
1. In a medium skillet, over med-high heat, fry bacon, set aside.
2. Add vegetables to the skillet and cook, stirring occasionally, until golden brown.
3. Cut bacon into pieces and return to skillet.
4. Top with cheese and allow it to melt. Serve immediately.

Nutrition:
- Calories 155
- Total Carbs 16 g
- Net Carbs 10 g
- Protein 10 g
- Fat 7 g
- Sugar 7 g
- Fiber 6 g

4. Cheese Spinach Waffles

Preparation time: 10 minutes
Cooking time: 20 minutes
Servings: 4
Ingredients:
- 2 strips of bacon, cooked and crumbled
- 2 eggs, lightly beaten

- 1/2 cup cauliflower, grated
- 1/2 cup frozen spinach, chopped (squeeze water out first)
- 1/2 cup low-fat mozzarella cheese, grated
- 1/2 cup low-fat cheddar cheese, grated
- 1 tbsp. margarine, melted

What you'll need from store cupboard:
- 1/4 cup reduced-fat Parmesan cheese, grated
- 1 tsp onion powder
- 1 tsp garlic powder
- Nonstick cooking spray

Directions:
1. Thaw spinach and squeeze out as much of the water as you, place in a large bowl.
2. Heat your waffle iron and spray with cooking spray.
3. Add remaining ingredients to the spinach and mix well.
4. Pour small amounts on the waffle iron and cook like you would for regular waffles. Serve warm.

Nutrition:
- Calories 186
- Total Carbs 2 g
- Protein 14 g
- Fat 14 g
- Sugar 1 g
- Fiber 0 g

5. Cinnamon Apple Granola

Preparation time: 5 minutes
Cooking time: 35 minutes
Servings: 4
Ingredients:
- 1 apple, peel and dice fine
- 1/4 cup margarine, melted

What you'll need from store cupboard:
- 1 cup walnuts or pecans
- 1 cup almond flour
- 3/4 cup flaked coconut
- 1/2 cup sunflower seeds
- 1/2 cup hemp seeds
- 1/3 cup Splenda
- 2 tsp cinnamon
- 2 tsp vanilla
- 1/2 tsp salt

Directions:
1. Heat oven to 300° F. Line a large baking sheet with parchment paper.
2. Place the nuts, flour, coconut, seeds, Splenda, and salt in a food processor. Pulse until mixture resembles coarse crumbs but leave some chunks.
3. Transfer to a bowl and add apple and cinnamon. Stir in margarine and vanilla until well coated and the mixture starts to clump together.
4. Pour onto prepared pan and spread out evenly. Bake 25 minutes, stirring a couple of times, until it starts to brown.
5. Turn the oven off and let the granola sit inside 5-10 minutes. Remove from oven and cool completely. It will crisp up more as it cools.
6. Store in an airtight container.

Nutrition:
- Calories 360
- Total Carbs 19 g
- Net Carbs 14 g
- Protein 10 g
- Fat 28 g
- Sugar 12 g
- Fiber 5 g

6. Coconut Breakfast Porridge

Preparation time: 2 minutes
Cooking time: 10 minutes
Servings: 4
Ingredients:
- 4 cup vanilla almond milk, unsweetened
- What you'll need from store cupboard:
- 1 cup unsweetened coconut, grated
- 8 tsp coconut flour

Directions:
1. Add coconut to a saucepan and cook over med-high heat until it is lightly toasted. Be careful not to let it burn.
2. Add milk and bring to a boil. While stirring slowly add flour, cook and stir until mixture starts to thicken, about 5 minutes.
3. Remove from heat, mixture will thicken more as it cools.

4. Ladle into bowls, add blueberries, or drizzle with a little honey if desired.

Nutrition:
- Calories 231
- Total Carbs 21 g
- Net Carbs 8 g
- Protein 6 g
- Fat 14 g
- Sugar 4 g
- Fiber 13 g

7. Cottage Cheese Pancakes

Preparation time: 5 minutes
Cooking time: 5 minutes
Servings: 2
Ingredients:
- 1 cup low-fat cottage cheese
- 4 egg whites

What you'll need from the store cupboard
- 1/2 cup oats
- 1 tbsp. Stevia, raw, optional
- 1 tsp vanilla
- Nonstick cooking spray

Directions:
1. Place all ingredients into a blender and process until smooth.
2. Spray a medium skillet with cooking spray and heat over medium heat.
3. Pour about 1/4 cup batter into a hot pan and cook until golden brown on both sides.
4. Serve with sugar-free syrup, fresh berries, or topping of your choice.

Nutrition:
- Calories 250
- Total carbs 25 g
- Net Carbs 23 g
- Protein 25 g
- Fat 4 g
- Sugar 7 g
- Fiber 2 g

8. Ham & Jicama Hash

Preparation time: 10 minutes
Cooking time: 15 minutes
Servings: 4
Ingredients:
- 6 eggs, beaten
- 2 cups jicama, grated
- 1 cup low-fat cheddar cheese, grated
- 1 cup ham, diced

What you'll need from store cupboard:
- Salt and pepper, to taste
- Nonstick cooking spray

Directions:
1. Spray a large nonstick skillet with cooking spray and place over medium-high heat. Add jicama and cook, stirring occasionally, until it starts to brown, about 5 minutes.
2. Add remaining ingredients and reduce heat to medium. Cook about 3 minutes, then flip over and cook until eggs are set, about 3-5 minutes more. Season with salt and pepper and serve.

Nutrition:
- Calories 221 Total Carbs 8 g
- Net Carbs 5 g Protein 21 g
- Fat 11 g Sugar 2 g Fiber 3 g

9. Hot Maple Porridge

Preparation time: 2 minutes
Cooking time: 1 minute
Servings: 1
Ingredients:
- 1 tsp margarine

What you'll need from store cupboard:
- 1/2 cup water
- 2 tbsp. flax meal
- 1 tbsp. almond flour
- 1 tbsp. coconut flour
- 1 tsp Splenda
- 1/4 tsp maple extract
- Pinch salt

Directions:
1. In a microwave safe bowl, combine all ingredients, except margarine, and mix thoroughly.
2. Microwave on high for one minute.
3. Stir in margarine and serve.

Nutrition:
- Calories 143
- Total Carbs 9 g
- Net Carbs 2 g
- Protein 5 g
- Fat 1 g
- Sugar 0 g
- Fiber 7 g

Jicama Hash Browns

Preparation time: 10 minutes
Cooking time: 20 minutes
Servings: 2
Ingredients:
- 2 cups jicama, peeled and grated
- 1/2 small onion, diced

What you'll need from the store cupboard:
- 1 tbsp. vegetable oil
- A pinch of salt to taste
- A pinch of pepper to taste

Directions:
1. Add the oil to a large skillet and heat over med-high heat.
2. Add the onion and cook until translucent.
3. Add the jicama and salt and pepper to taste. Cook until nicely browned on both sides. Serve immediately.

Nutrition:
- Calories 113 Total Carbs 12 g
- Net Carbs 6 g
- Protein 1 g
- Fat 7 g
- Sugar 3 g
- Fiber 6 g

10.   Blueberry Breakfast Cake

Preparation time: 15 minutes
Cooking time: 45 minutes
Servings: 12
Ingredients:
For the topping:
- 1/4 cup finely chopped walnuts
- 1/2 teaspoon ground cinnamon
- 2 tablespoons butter, chopped into small pieces
- 2 tablespoons sugar

For the cake:
- Nonstick cooking spray
- 1 cup whole-wheat pastry flour
- 1 cup oat flour
- 1/4 cup sugar
- 2 teaspoons baking powder
- 1 large egg beaten
- 1/2 cup skim milk
- 2 tablespoons butter, melted
- 1 teaspoon grated lemon peel
- 2 cups fresh or frozen blueberries

Directions:
To make the topping:
1. In a small bowl, stir together the walnuts, cinnamon, butter, and sugar. Set aside.

To make the cake:
1. Preheat the oven to 350°F. Spray a 9-inch square pan with cooking spray. Set aside.
2. In a large bowl, stir together the pastry flour, oat flour, sugar, and baking powder.
3. Add the egg milk, butter, and lemon peel, and stir until there are no dry spots.
4. Stir in the blueberries, and gently mix until incorporated. Press the batter into the prepared pan, using a spoon to flatten it into the dish.
5. Sprinkle the topping over the cake.
6. Bake for 40 to 45 minutes, until a toothpick inserted into the cake comes out clean, and serve.

Nutrition:
- Calories: 177;
- Total Fat: 7 g
- Saturated Fat: 3 g
- Protein: 4 g
- Carbohydrates: 26 g
- Sugar: 9 g
- Fiber: 3 g
- Cholesterol: 26 mg

- Sodium: 39 mg

11.   Whole-grain Pancakes

Preparation time: 10 minutes
Cooking time: 15 minutes
Servings: 4 to 6
Ingredients:
- 2 cups whole-wheat pastry flour
- 4 teaspoons baking powder
- 2 teaspoons ground cinnamon
- 1/2 teaspoon salt
- 2 cups skim milk, plus more as needed
- 2 large eggs
- 1 tablespoon honey
- Nonstick cooking spray
- Maple syrup, for serving
- Fresh fruit, for serving

Directions:
1. In a large bowl, stir together the flour, baking powder, cinnamon, and salt.
2. Add the milk, eggs, and honey, and stir well to combine. If needed, add more milk, 1 tablespoon at a time, until there are no dry spots and you have a pourable batter.
3. Heat a large skillet over medium-high heat, and spray it with cooking spray.
4. Using a 1/4-cup measuring cup, scoop 2 or 3 pancakes into the skillet at a time. Cook for a couple of minutes, until bubbles form on the surface of the pancakes, flip, and cook for 1 to 2 minutes more, until golden brown and cooked through. Repeat with the remaining batter.
5. Serve topped with maple syrup or fresh fruit.

Nutrition:
- Calories: 392;
- Total Fat: 4 g
- Saturated Fat: 1 g
- Protein: 15 g
- Carbohydrates: 71 g
- Sugar: 11 g
- Fiber: 9 g

12. Buckwheat Grouts Breakfast Bowl

Preparation time: 5 minutes, plus overnight to soak
Cooking time: 10 to 12 minutes
Servings: 4
Ingredients:
- 3 cups skim milk
- 1 cup buckwheat grouts
- 1/4 cup chia seeds
- 2 teaspoons vanilla extract
- 1/2 teaspoon ground cinnamon
- Pinch salt
- 1 cup water
- 1/2 cup unsalted pistachios
- 2 cups sliced fresh strawberries
- 1/4 cup cacao nibs (optional)

Directions:
1. In a large bowl, stir together the milk, groats, chia seeds, vanilla, cinnamon, and salt. Cover and refrigerate overnight.
2. The following day, transfer the soaked mixture to a medium pot and add the water. Bring to a boil over medium-high heat, reduce the heat to maintain a simmer, and cook for 10 to 12 minutes until the buckwheat is tender and thickened.
3. Transfer to bowls and serve, topped with the pistachios, strawberries, and cacao nibs (if using).

Nutrition:
- Calories: 340;
- Total Fat: 8 g
- Saturated Fat: 1 g
- Protein: 15 g
- Carbohydrates: 52 g
- Sugar: 14 g
- Fiber: 10 g
- Cholesterol: 4 mg
- Sodium: 140 mg

13. Peach Muesli Bake

Preparation time: 10 minutes
Cooking time: 40 minutes
Servings: 8
Ingredients:
- Nonstick cooking spray
- 2 cups skim milk
- 1 ½ cup rolled oats
- 1/2 cup chopped walnuts
- 1 large egg
- 2 tablespoons maple syrup
- 1 teaspoon ground cinnamon
- 1 teaspoon baking powder
- 1/2 teaspoon salt
- 2 to 3 peaches, sliced

Directions:
1. Preheat the oven to 375° F. Spray a 9-inch square baking dish with cooking spray. Set aside.
2. In a large bowl, stir together the milk, oats, walnuts, egg maple syrup, cinnamon, baking powder, and salt. Spread half the mixture in the prepared baking dish.
3. Place half the peaches in a single layer across the oat mixture.
4. Spread the remaining oat mixture over the top. Add the remaining peaches in a thin layer over the oats. Bake for 35 to 40 minutes, uncovered, until thickened and browned.

5. Cut into 8 squares and serve warm.

Nutrition:
- Calories: 138; Total Fat: 3 g
- Saturated Fat: 1 g Protein: 6 g
- Carbohydrates: 22 g
- Sugar: 10 g
- Fiber: 3 g
- Cholesterol: 24mg
- Sodium: 191mg

14. Steel-Cut Oatmeal Bowl with Fruit and Nuts

Preparation time: 5 minutes
Cooking time: 20 minutes
Servings: 4
Ingredients:
- 1 cup steel-cut oats
- 2 cups almond milk
- 3/4 cup water
- 1 teaspoon ground cinnamon
- 1/4 teaspoon salt
- 2 cups chopped fresh fruit, such as blueberries, strawberries, raspberries, or peaches
- 1/2 cup chopped walnuts
- 1/4 cup chia seeds

Directions:
1. In a medium saucepan over medium-high heat, combine the oats, almond milk, water, cinnamon, and salt. Bring to a boil, reduce the heat to low, and simmer for 15 to 20 minutes, until the oats are softened and thickened.
2. Top each bowl with 1/2 cup of fresh fruit, 2 tablespoons of walnuts, and 1 tablespoon of chia seeds before serving.

Nutrition:
- Calories: 288;
- Total Fat: 11 g
- Saturated Fat: 1 g
- Protein: 10 g
- Carbohydrates: 38 g
- Sugar: 7 g
- Fiber: 10 g
- Cholesterol: 0 mg
- Sodium: 329 mg

15. Whole-Grain Dutch Baby Pancake

Preparation time: 5 minutes
Cooking time: 25 minutes
Servings: 4
Ingredients:
- 2 tablespoons coconut oil
- 1/2 cup whole-wheat flour
- 1/4 cup skim milk
- 3 large eggs
- 1 teaspoon vanilla extract
- 1/2 teaspoon baking powder
- 1/4 teaspoon salt
- 1/4 teaspoon ground cinnamon
- Powdered sugar, for dusting

Directions:
1. Preheat the oven to 400° F.
2. Put the coconut oil in a medium oven-safe skillet, and place the skillet in the oven to melt the oil while it preheats.
3. In a blender, combine the flour, milk, eggs, vanilla, baking powder, salt, and cinnamon. Process until smooth.
4. Carefully remove the skillet from the oven and tilt to spread the oil around evenly.
5. Pour the batter into the skillet and return it to the oven for 23 to 25 minutes, until the pancake puffs and lightly browns.
6. Remove, dust lightly with powdered sugar, cut into 4 wedges, and serve.

Nutrition:
- Calories: 195;
- Total Fat: 11 g
- Saturated Fat: 7 g
- Protein: 8 g
- Carbohydrates: 16 g
- Sugar: 1 g
- Fiber: 2 g
- Cholesterol: 140 mg
- Sodium: 209 mg

16. Mushroom, Zucchini, and Onion Frittata

Preparation time: 10 minutes
Cooking time: 20 minutes
Servings: 4
Ingredients:
- 1 tablespoon extra-virgin olive oil

- 1/2 onion, chopped
- 1 medium zucchini, chopped
- 1 ½ cup sliced mushrooms
- 6 large eggs, beaten
- 2 tablespoons skim milk
- Salt
- Freshly ground black pepper
- 1 ounce feta cheese, crumbled

Directions:
1. Preheat the oven to 400° F.
2. In a medium oven-safe skillet over medium-high heat, heat the olive oil.
3. Add the onion and sauté for 3 to 5 minutes, until translucent.
4. Add the zucchini and mushrooms, and cook for 3 to 5 more minutes, until the vegetables are tender.
5. Meanwhile, in a small bowl, whisk the eggs, milk, salt, and pepper. Pour the mixture into the skillet, stirring to combine, and transfer the skillet to the oven. Cook for 7 to 9 minutes, until set.
6. Sprinkle with the feta cheese, and cook for 1 to 2 minutes more, until heated through.
7. Remove, cut into 4 wedges, and serve.

Nutrition:
- Calories: 178;
- Total Fat: 13 g
- Saturated Fat: 4 g
- Protein: 12 g
- Carbohydrates: 5 g
- Sugar: 3 g
- Fiber: 1 g
- Cholesterol: 285 mg
- Sodium: 234 mg

17.   Spinach and Cheese Quiche

Preparation time: 10 minutes, plus 10 minutes to rest
Cooking time: 50 minutes
Servings: 4 to 6
Ingredients:
- Nonstick cooking spray
- 8 ounces yukon gold potatoes, shredded
- 1 tablespoon plus 2 teaspoons extra-virgin olive oil, divided
- 1 teaspoon salt, divided
- Freshly ground black pepper
- 1 onion, finely chopped
- 1 (10-ounce) bag fresh spinach
- 4 large eggs
- 1/2 cup skim milk
- 1 ounce gruyere cheese, shredded

Directions:
1. Preheat the oven to 350° F. Spray a 9-inch pie dish with cooking spray. Set aside.
2. In a small bowl, toss the potatoes with 2 teaspoons of olive oil, 1/2 teaspoon of salt, and season with pepper. Press the potatoes into the bottom and sides of the pie dish to form a thin, even layer. Bake for 20 minutes, until golden brown. Remove from the oven and set aside to cool.
3. In a large skillet over medium-high heat, heat the remaining 1 tablespoon of olive oil.
4. Add the onion and sauté for 3 to 5 minutes, until softened.
5. By handfuls, add the spinach, stirring between each addition, until it just starts to wilt before adding more. Cook for about 1 minute, until it cooks down.
6. In a medium bowl, whisk the eggs and milk. Add the gruyere, and season with the remaining 1/2 teaspoon of salt and some pepper. Fold the eggs into the spinach. Pour the mixture into the pie dish and bake for 25 minutes, until the eggs are set.
7. Let rest for 10 minutes before serving.

Nutrition:
- Calories: 445;
- Total Fat: 14 g
- Saturated Fat: 4 g
- Protein: 19 g
- Carbohydrates: 68 g
- Sugar: 6 g
- Fiber: 7 g
- Cholesterol: 193 mg
- Sodium: 773 mg

18.   Spicy Jalapeno Popper Deviled Eggs

Preparation time: 5 minutes
Cooking time: 5 minutes
Servings: 4
Ingredients:
- 4 large whole eggs, hardboiled
- 2 tablespoons Keto-Friendly mayonnaise

- 1/4 cup cheddar cheese, grated
- 2 slices bacon, cooked and crumbled
- 1 jalapeno, sliced

Directions:
1. Cut eggs in half, remove the yolk and put them in a bowl
2. Lay egg whites on a platter
3. Mix in the remaining ingredients and mash them with the egg yolks
4. Transfer yolk mix back to the egg whites
5. Serve and enjoy!

Nutrition:
- Calories: 176;
- Fat: 14 g
- Carbohydrates: 0.7 g
- Protein: 10 g

19. Lovely Porridge

Preparation time: 5 minutes
Cooking time: 10 minutes
Servings: 2
Ingredients:
- 2 tablespoons coconut flour
- 2 tablespoons vanilla protein powder
- 3 tablespoons Golden Flaxseed meal
- 1 and 1/2 cups almond milk, unsweetened
- Powdered erythritol

Directions:
1. Take a bowl and mix in flaxseed meal, protein powder, coconut flour and mix well
2. Add mix to the saucepan (placed over medium heat)
3. Add almond milk and stir, let the mixture thicken
4. Add your desired amount of sweetener and serve
5. Enjoy!

Nutrition:
- Calories: 259;
- Fat: 13 g
- Carbohydrates: 5 g
- Protein: 16 g

CHAPTER 6:

Lunch Recipes

20. Asparagus with Scallops

Preparation time: 10 minutes
Cooking time: 15 minutes
Servings: 4
Ingredients:
- 1 pound (454 g) asparagus, trimmed and cut into 2-inch segments
- 1 pound (454 g) sea scallops
- 1/4 cup dry white wine
- Juice of 1 lemon
- 2 garlic cloves, minced

From the Cupboard:
- 3 teaspoons extra-virgin olive oil, divided
- 1 tablespoon butter
- 1/4 teaspoon freshly ground black pepper

Directions:
1. In a large skillet, heat 1 ½ teaspoon of oil over medium heat.
2. Add the asparagus and sauté for 5 to 6 minutes until just tender, stirring regularly. Remove from the skillet and cover with aluminum foil to keep warm.
3. Add the remaining 1 ½ teaspoon of oil and the butter to the skillet. When the butter is melted and sizzling place the scallops in a single layer in the skillet. Cook for about 3 minutes on one side until nicely browned. Use tongs to gently loosen and flip the scallops, and cook on the other side for another 3 minutes until browned and cooked through. Remove and cover with foil to keep warm.
4. In the same skillet, combine the wine, lemon juice, garlic, and pepper. Bring to a simmer for 1 to 2 minutes, stirring to mix in any browned pieces left in the pan.
5. Return the asparagus and the cooked scallops to the skillet to coat with the sauce. Serve warm.

Nutrition:
- Calories: 253
- Fat: 7.1 g
- Protein: 26.1 g
- Carbohydrates: 14.9 g
- Fiber: 2.1 g
- Sugar: 3.1 g
- Sodium: 494 mg

21. Butter Cod with Asparagus

Preparation time: 5 minutes
Cooking time: 10 minutes
Servings: 4
Ingredients:
- 4 (4-ounce / 113-g) cod fillets
- 1/4 teaspoon garlic powder
- 24 asparagus spears, woody ends trimmed
- 1/2 cup brown rice, cooked
- 1 tablespoon freshly squeezed lemon juice

From the Cupboard:
- 1/4 teaspoon salt
- 1/4 teaspoon freshly ground black pepper
- 2 tablespoons unsalted butter

Directions:
1. In a large bowl, season the cod fillets with the garlic powder, salt, and pepper. Set aside.
2. Melt the butter in a skillet over medium-low heat.
3. Place the cod fillets and asparagus in the skillet in a single layer. Cook covered for 8 minutes, or until the cod is cooked through.
4. Divide the cooked brown rice, cod fillets, and asparagus among four plates. Serve drizzled with the lemon juice.

Nutrition:
- Calories: 233
- Fat: 8.2 g
- Protein: 22.1 g
- Carbohydrates: 20.1 g
- Fiber: 5.2 g
- Sugar: 2.2 g
- Sodium: 275 mg

22. Creamy Cod Fillet with Quinoa and Asparagus

Preparation time: 5 minutes
Cooking time: 15 minutes
Servings: 4
Ingredients:
- 1/2 cup uncooked quinoa
- 4 (4-ounce / 113-g) cod fillets
- 1/2 teaspoon garlic powder, divided
- 24 asparagus spears, cut the bottom 1 ½ inch off
- 1 cup half-and-half

From the Cupboard:
- 1/4 teaspoon salt
- 1/4 teaspoon freshly ground black pepper
- 1 tablespoon avocado oil

Directions:
1. Put the quinoa in a pot of salted water. Bring to a boil. Reduce the heat to low and simmer for 15 minutes or until the quinoa is soft and has a white "tail." Cover and turn off the heat. Let sit for 5 minutes.
2. On a clean work surface, rub the cod fillets with 1/4 teaspoon of garlic powder, salt, and pepper.
3. Heat the avocado oil in a nonstick skillet over medium-low heat.
4. Add the cod fillets and asparagus in the skillet and cook for 8 minutes or until they are tender. Flip the cod and shake the skillet halfway through the cooking time.
5. Pour the half-and-half in the skillet, and sprinkle with remaining garlic powder. Turn up the heat to high and simmer for 2 minutes until creamy.
6. Divide the quinoa, cod fillets, and asparagus in four bowls and serve warm.

Nutrition:
- Calories: 258
- Fat: 7.9 g
- Protein: 25.2 g
- Carbohydrates: 22.7 g
- Fiber: 5.2 g
- Sugar: 3.8 g
- Sodium: 410 mg

23. Asparagus and Scallop Skillet With Lemony

Preparation time: 10 minutes
Cooking time: 15 minutes
Servings: 4
Ingredients:
- 1 pound (454 g) asparagus, trimmed and cut into 2-inch segments
- 1 pound (454 g) sea scallops
- 1/4 cup dry white wine
- 2 garlic cloves, minced
- Juice of 1 lemon

From the Cupboard:
- 3 teaspoons extra-virgin olive oil, divided
- 1 tablespoon butter
- 1/4 teaspoon freshly ground black pepper

Directions:
1. Heat half of olive oil in a nonstick skillet over medium heat until shimmering.
2. Add the asparagus to the skillet and sauté for 6 minutes until soft. Transfer the cooked asparagus to a large plate and cover it with aluminum foil.
3. Heat the remaining half of olive oil and butter in the skillet until the butter is melted.
4. Add the scallops to the skillet and cook for 6 minutes or until opaque and browned. Flip the scallops with tongs halfway through the cooking time. Transfer the scallops to the plate and cover them with aluminum foil.
5. Combine the wine, garlic, lemon juice, and black pepper in the skillet. Simmer over medium-low heat for 2 minutes. Keep stirring during the simmering.
6. Pour the sauce over the asparagus and scallops to coat well, then serve warm.

Nutrition:
- Calories: 256
- Fat: 6.9 g
- Protein: 26.1 g
- Carbohydrates: 14.9 g
- Fiber: 2.1 g
- Sugar: 2.9 g
- Sodium: 491 mg

24. Butter-Lemon Grilled Cod on Asparagus

Preparation time: 5 minutes
Cooking time: 9 to 12 minutes
Servings: 4
Ingredients:
- 1 pound (454 g) asparagus spears, ends trimmed
- 4 (4-ounce / 113-g) cod fillets, rinsed and patted dry
- Juice and zest of 1 medium lemon

From the Cupboard:
- Cooking spray
- 1/4 teaspoon black pepper (optional)
- 1/4 cup light butter with canola oil
- 1/4 teaspoon salt (optional)

Directions:
1. Heat a grill pan over medium-high heat.
2. Spray the asparagus spears with cooking spray. Cook the asparagus for 6 to 8 minutes until fork-tender, flipping occasionally.
3. Transfer to a large platter and keep warm.
4. Spray both sides of fillets with cooking spray. Season with 1/4 teaspoon black pepper, if needed. Add the fillets to the pan and sear each side for 3 minutes until opaque.
5. Meantime, in a small bowl, whisk together the light butter, lemon zest, and 1/4 teaspoon salt (if desired).
6. Spoon and spread the mixture all over the asparagus. Place the fish on top and squeeze the lemon juice over the fish. Serve immediately.

Nutrition:
- Calories: 158
- Fat: 6.4 g
- Protein: 23.0 g
- Carbohydrates: 6.1 g
- Fiber: 3.0 g
- Sugar: 2.8 g
- Sodium: 212 mg

25. Lemon Parsley White Fish Fillets

Preparation time: 10 minutes
Cooking time: 10 minutes
Servings: 4
Ingredients:
- 4 (6-ounce / 170-g) lean white fish fillets, rinsed and patted dry
- 2 tablespoons parsley, finely chopped
- 1/2 teaspoon lemon zest
- 1/4 teaspoon dried dill
- 1 medium lemon, halved

From the Cupboard:
- Cooking spray
- Paprika, to taste
- Salt and pepper, to taste
- 1/4 cup extra virgin olive oil

Directions:
1. Preheat the oven to 400°F (205°C). Line a baking sheet with aluminum foil and spray with cooking spray.
2. Place the fillets on the foil and scatter with the paprika. Season as desired with salt and pepper.
3. Bake in the preheated oven for 10 minutes, or until the flesh flakes easily with a fork.
4. Meanwhile, stir together the parsley, lemon zest, olive oil, and dill in a small bowl.
5. Remove the fish from the oven to four plates. Squeeze the lemon juice over the fish and serve topped with the parsley mixture.

Nutrition:
- Calories: 283 Fat: 17.2 g
- Protein: 33.3 g Carbohydrates: 1.0 g
- Fiber: 0 g Sugar: 0 g Sodium: 74 mg

26. Cilantro Lime Shrimp

Preparation time: 15 minutes
Cooking time: 8 minutes
Servings: 4
Ingredients:
- 1/2 teaspoon garlic clove, minced
- 1 pound (454 g) large shrimp, peeled and deveined
- 1/4 cup chopped fresh cilantro, or more to taste
- 1 lime, zested and juiced

From the Cupboard:
- 1 teaspoon extra virgin olive oil
- 1/4 teaspoon salt
- 1/8 teaspoon black pepper

Directions:
1. In a large, heavy skillet, heat the olive oil over medium-high heat.
2. Add the minced garlic and cook for 30 seconds until fragrant.
3. Toss in the shrimp and cook for about 5 to 6 minutes, stirring occasionally, or until they turn pink and opaque.
4. Remove from the heat to a bowl. Add the cilantro, lime zest and juice, salt, and pepper to the shrimp, and toss to combine. Serve immediately.

Nutrition:
- Calories: 133
- Fat: 3.5 g
- Protein: 24.3 g
- Carbohydrates: 1.0 g
- Fiber: 0 g
- Sugar: 0 g
- Sodium: 258 mg

27. Cajun Catfish

Preparation time: 5 minutes
Cooking time: 15 minutes
Servings: 4
Ingredients:
- 4 (8-ounce / 227-g) catfish fillets
- 2 teaspoons thyme
- 1/2 teaspoon red hot sauce

From the Cupboard:
- 2 tablespoons olive oil
- 2 teaspoons garlic salt
- 2 teaspoons paprika
- 1/2 teaspoon cayenne pepper
- 1/4 teaspoon black pepper
- Nonstick cooking spray

Directions:
1. Heat oven to 450°F (235°C). Spray a baking dish with cooking spray.
2. In a small bowl, whisk together everything but catfish. Brush both sides of fillets, using all the spice mix.
3. Bake 10 to 13 minutes or until fish flakes easily with a fork. Serve.

Nutrition:
- Calories: 367
- Fat: 24.0 g
- Protein: 35.2 g
- Carbohydrates: 0 g
- Fiber: 0 g
- Sugar: 0 g
- Sodium: 70 mg

28. Tomato Tuna Melts

Preparation time: 5 minutes
Cooking time: 5 minutes
Servings: 2
Ingredients:
- 1 (5-ounce) can chunk light tuna packed in water, drained
- 2 tablespoons plain nonfat Greek yogurt
- 2 teaspoons freshly squeezed lemon juice
- 2 tablespoons finely chopped celery
- 1 tablespoon finely chopped red onion
- Pinch cayenne pepper
- 1 large tomato, cut into 3/4-inch-thick rounds
- 1/2 cup shredded cheddar cheese

Directions:
1. Preheat the broiler to high.
2. In a medium bowl, combine the tuna, yogurt, lemon juice, celery, red onion, and cayenne pepper. Stir well.
3. Arrange the tomato slices on a baking sheet. Top each with some tuna salad and cheddar cheese.
4. Broil for 3 to 4 minutes until the cheese is melted and bubbly. Serve.

Nutrition:
- Calories: 243;
- Total Fat: 10 g
- Protein: 30 g
- Carbohydrates: 7 g
- Sugars: 2 g
- Fiber: 1 g
- Sodium: 444 mg

29. Peppercorn-Crusted Baked Salmon

Preparation time: 5 minutes
Cooking time: 20 minutes
Servings: 4
Ingredients:
- Nonstick cooking spray
- 1/2 teaspoon freshly ground black pepper
- 1/4 teaspoon salt
- Zest and juice of 1/2 lemon
- 1/4 teaspoon dried thyme
- 1 pound salmon fillet

Directions:
1. Preheat the oven to 425°F. Spray a baking sheet with nonstick cooking spray.
2. In a small bowl, combine the pepper, salt, lemon zest and juice, and thyme. Stir to combine.
3. Place the salmon on the prepared baking sheet, skin-side down. Spread the seasoning mixture evenly over the fillet.
4. Bake for 15 to 20 minutes, depending on the thickness of the fillet, until the flesh flakes easily.

Nutrition:
- Calories: 163; Total Fat: 7 g
- Protein: 23 g Carbohydrates: 1 g
- Sugars: 0 g Fiber: 0 g Sodium: 167 mg

30. Roasted Salmon with Honey-Mustard Sauce

Preparation time: 5 minutes
Cooking time: 20 minutes
Servings: 4
Ingredients:
- Nonstick cooking spray
- 2 tablespoons whole-grain mustard
- 1 tablespoon honey
- 2 garlic cloves, minced
- 1/4 teaspoon salt
- 1/4 teaspoon freshly ground black pepper
- 1 pound salmon fillet

Directions:
1. Preheat the oven to 425°F. Spray a baking sheet with nonstick cooking spray.
2. In a small bowl, whisk together the mustard, honey, garlic, salt, and pepper.
3. Place the salmon fillet on the prepared baking sheet, skin-side down. Spoon the sauce onto the salmon and spread evenly.
4. Roast for 15 to 20 minutes, depending on the thickness of the fillet, until the flesh flakes easily.

Nutrition:
- Calories: 186;
- Total Fat: 7 g
- Protein: 23 g
- Carbohydrates: 6 g
- Sugars: 4 g
- Fiber: 0 g
- Sodium: 312 mg

31. Ginger-Glazed Salmon and Broccoli

Preparation time: 10 minutes
Cooking time: 15 minutes
Servings: 4
Ingredients:
- Nonstick cooking spray
- 1 tablespoon low-sodium tamari or gluten-free soy sauce
- Juice of 1 lemon
- 1 tablespoon honey
- 1 (1-inch) piece fresh ginger, grated
- 1 garlic clove, minced
- 1 pound salmon fillet
- 1/4 teaspoon salt, divided
- 1/8 teaspoon freshly ground black pepper
- 2 broccoli heads, cut into florets
- 1 tablespoon extra-virgin olive oil

Directions:
1. Preheat the oven to 400°F. Spray a baking sheet with nonstick cooking spray.
2. In a small bowl, mix the tamari, lemon juice, honey, ginger, and garlic. Set aside.
3. Place the salmon skin-side down on the prepared baking sheet. Season with 1/8 teaspoon of salt and pepper.
4. In a large mixing bowl, toss the broccoli and olive oil. Season with the remaining 1/8 teaspoon of salt. Arrange in a single layer on the baking sheet next to the salmon. Bake for 15 to 20 minutes until the salmon flakes easily with a fork and the broccoli is fork-tender.
5. In a small pan over medium heat, bring the tamari-ginger mixture to a simmer and cook for 1 to 2 minutes until it just begins to thicken.
6. Drizzle the sauce over the salmon and serve.

Nutrition:
- Calories: 238;
- Total Fat: 11 g
- Protein: 25 g
- Carbohydrates: 11 g
- Sugars: 6 g
- Fiber: 2 g
- Sodium: 334 mg

32. Roasted Salmon with Salsa Verde

Preparation time: 5 minutes
Cooking time: 25 minutes
Servings: 4
Ingredients:
- Nonstick cooking spray
- 8 ounces tomatillos, husks removed
- 1/2 onion, quartered
- 1 jalapeño or serrano pepper, seeded
- 1 garlic clove, unpeeled
- 1 teaspoon extra-virgin olive oil
- 1/2 teaspoon salt, divided
- 4 (4-ounce) wild-caught salmon fillets
- 1/4 teaspoon freshly ground black pepper
- 1/4 cup chopped fresh cilantro
- Juice of 1 lime

Directions:
1. Preheat the oven to 425°F. Spray a baking sheet with nonstick cooking spray.
2. In a large bowl, toss the tomatillos, onion, jalapeño, garlic, olive oil, and 1/4 teaspoon of salt to coat. Arrange in a single layer on the prepared baking sheet, and roast for about 10 minutes until just softened. Transfer to a dish or plate and set aside.
3. Arrange the salmon fillets skin-side down on the same baking sheet, and season with the remaining 1/4 teaspoon of salt and pepper. Bake for 12 to 15 minutes until the fish is firm and flakes easily.
4. Meanwhile, peel the roasted garlic and place it and the roasted vegetables in a blender or food processor. Add a scant 1/4 cup of water to the jar, and process until smooth.
5. Add the cilantro and lime juice and process until smooth. Serve the salmon topped with the salsa verde.

Nutrition:
- Calories: 199; Total Fat: 9 g
- Protein: 23 g
- Carbohydrates: 6 g
- Sugars: 3 g
- Fiber: 2 g
- Sodium: 295 mg

33. Whole Veggie-Stuffed Trout

Preparation time: 10 minutes
Cooking time: 25 minutes
Servings: 2
Ingredients:
- Nonstick cooking spray
- 2 (8-ounce) whole trout fillets, dressed (cleaned but with bones and skin intact)
- 1 tablespoon extra-virgin olive oil
- 1/4 teaspoon salt
- 1/8 teaspoon freshly ground black pepper
- 1/2 red bell pepper, seeded and thinly sliced
- 1 small onion, thinly sliced
- 2 or 3 shiitake mushrooms, sliced
- 1 poblano pepper, seeded and thinly sliced
- 1 lemon, sliced

Directions:
1. Preheat the oven to 425°F. Spray a baking sheet with nonstick cooking spray.
2. Rub both trout, inside and out, with the olive oil, then season with the salt and pepper.
3. In a large bowl, combine the bell pepper, onion, mushrooms, and poblano pepper. Stuff half of this mixture into the cavity of each fish. Top the mixture with 2 or 3 lemon slices inside each fish.
4. Arrange the fish on the prepared baking sheet side by side and roast for 25 minutes until the fish is cooked through and the vegetables are tender.

Nutrition:
- Calories: 452;
- Total Fat: 22 g
- Protein: 49 g
- Carbohydrates: 14 g
- Sugars: 5 g
- Fiber: 3 g

34. Ginger-Garlic Cod Cooked in Paper

Preparation time: 10 minutes
Cooking time: 15 minutes
Servings: 4
Ingredients:
- 1 chard bunch, stemmed, leaves and stems cut into thin strips
- 1 red bell pepper, seeded and cut into strips
- 1 pound cod fillets cut into 4 pieces
- 1 tablespoon grated fresh ginger
- 3 garlic cloves, minced
- 2 tablespoons white wine vinegar
- 2 tablespoons low-sodium tamari or gluten-free soy sauce
- 1 tablespoon honey

Directions:
1. Preheat the oven to 425°F.
2. Cut four pieces of parchment paper, each about 16 inches wide. Lay the four pieces out on a large workspace.
3. On each piece of paper, arrange a small pile of chard leaves and stems, topped by several strips of bell pepper. Top with a piece of cod.
4. In a small bowl, mix the ginger, garlic, vinegar, tamari, and honey. Top each piece of fish with one-fourth of the mixture.

5. Fold the parchment paper over so the edges overlap. Fold the edges over several times to secure the fish in the packets. Carefully place the packets on a large baking sheet.
6. Bake for 12 minutes. Carefully open the packets, allowing steam to escape, and serve.

Nutrition:
- Calories: 118;
- Total Fat: 1 g
- Protein: 19 g
- Carbohydrates: 9 g
- Sugars: 6 g
- Fiber: 1 g
- Sodium: 715 mg

35. Roasted Halibut with Red Peppers, Green Beans, and Onions

Preparation time: 10 minutes
Cooking time: 15 minutes
Servings: 4
Ingredients:
- 1 pound green beans, trimmed
- 2 red bell peppers, seeded and cut into strips
- 1 onion, sliced
- Zest and juice of 2 lemons
- 3 garlic cloves, minced
- 2 tablespoons extra-virgin olive oil
- 1 teaspoon dried dill
- 1 teaspoon dried oregano
- 4 (4-ounce) halibut fillets
- 1/2 teaspoon salt
- 1/4 teaspoon freshly ground black pepper

Directions:
1. Preheat the oven to 400°F. Line a baking sheet with parchment paper.
2. In a large bowl, toss the green beans, bell peppers, onion, lemon zest and juice, garlic, olive oil, dill, and oregano.
3. Use a slotted spoon to transfer the vegetables to the prepared baking sheet in a single layer, leaving the juice behind in the bowl.
4. Gently place the halibut fillets in the bowl, and coat in the juice. Transfer the fillets to the baking sheet, nestled between the vegetables, and drizzle them with any juice left in the bowl. Sprinkle the vegetables and halibut with the salt and pepper.
5. Bake for 15 to 20 minutes until the vegetables are just tender and the fish flakes apart easily.

Nutrition:
- Calories: 234;
- Total Fat: 9 g
- Protein: 24 g
- Carbohydrates: 16 g
- Sugars: 8 g
- Fiber: 5 g

36. Blackened Tilapia with Mango Salsa

Preparation time: 15 minutes
Cooking time: 10 minutes
Servings: 2
Ingredients:
For the salsa:
- 1 cup chopped mango
- 2 tablespoons chopped red onion
- 2 tablespoons chopped fresh cilantro
- 2 tablespoons freshly squeezed lime juice
- 1/2 jalapeño pepper, seeded and minced
- Pinch salt

For the tilapia:
- 1 tablespoon paprika
- 1 teaspoon onion powder
- 1/2 teaspoon freshly ground black pepper
- 1/2 teaspoon dried thyme
- 1/2 teaspoon garlic powder
- 1/4 teaspoon cayenne pepper
- 1/4 teaspoon salt
- 1/2 pound boneless tilapia fillets
- 2 teaspoons extra-virgin olive oil
- 1 lime, cut into wedges, for serving

Directions:
To make the salsa:
1. In a medium bowl, toss together the mango, onion, cilantro, lime juice, jalapeño, and salt. Set aside.

To make the tilapia
1. In a small bowl, mix the paprika, onion powder, pepper, thyme, garlic powder, cayenne, and salt. Rub the mixture on both sides of the tilapia fillets.
2. In a large skillet, heat the oil over medium heat, and cook the fish for 3 to 5 minutes on each side until the outer coating is crisp and the fish is cooked through.

3. Spoon half of the salsa over each fillet and serve with lime wedges on the side.

Nutrition:
- Calories: 240;
- Total Fat: 8 g
- Protein: 25 g
- Carbohydrates: 22 g
- Sugars: 13 g
- Fiber: 4 g

37. Scallops and Asparagus Skillet

Preparation time: 10 minutes
Cooking time: 15 minutes
Servings: 4
Ingredients:
- 3 teaspoons extra-virgin olive oil, divided
- 1 pound asparagus, trimmed and cut into 2-inch segments
- 1 tablespoon butter
- 1 pound sea scallops
- 1/4 cup dry white wine
- Juice of 1 lemon
- 2 garlic cloves, minced
- 1/4 teaspoon freshly ground black pepper

Directions:
1. In a large skillet, heat 1 ½ teaspoons of oil over medium heat.
2. Add the asparagus and sauté for 5 to 6 minutes until just tender, stirring regularly. Remove from the skillet and cover with aluminum foil to keep warm.
3. Add the remaining 1 ½ teaspoons of oil and the butter to the skillet. When the butter is melted and sizzling place the scallops in a single layer in the skillet. Cook for about 3 minutes on one side until nicely browned. Use tongs to gently loosen and flip the scallops, and cook on the other side for another 3 minutes until browned and cooked through. Remove and cover with foil to keep warm.
4. In the same skillet, combine the wine, lemon juice, garlic, and pepper. Bring to a simmer for 1 to 2 minutes, stirring to mix in any browned pieces left in the pan.
5. Return the asparagus and the cooked scallops to the skillet to coat with the sauce. Serve warm.

Nutrition:
- Calories: 252;
- Total Fat: 7 g
- Protein: 26 g
- Carbohydrates: 15 g
- Sugars: 3 g
- Fiber: 2 g

38. Baked Oysters

Preparation time: 30 minutes
Cooking time: 15 minutes
Servings: 2
Ingredients:
- 2 cups coarse salt, for holding the oysters
- 1 dozen fresh oysters, scrubbed
- 1 tablespoon butter
- 1/2 cup finely chopped artichoke hearts
- 1/4 cup finely chopped scallions, both white and green parts
- 1/4 cup finely chopped red bell pepper
- 1 garlic clove, minced
- 1 tablespoon finely chopped fresh parsley
- Zest and juice of 1/2 lemon
- Pinch salt
- Freshly ground black pepper

Directions:
1. Pour the coarse salt into an 8-by-8-inch baking dish and spread to evenly fill the bottom of the dish.
2. Prepare a clean surface to shuck the oysters. Using a shucking knife, insert the blade at the joint of the shell, where it hinges open and shut. Firmly apply pressure to pop the blade in, and work the knife around the shell to open. Discard the empty half of the shell. Use the knife to gently loosen the oyster, and remove any shell particles. Set the oysters in their shells on the salt, being careful not to spill the juices.
3. Preheat the oven to 425°F.
4. In a large skillet, melt the butter over medium heat. Add the artichoke hearts, scallions, and bell pepper, and cook for 5 to 7 minutes. Add the garlic and cook an additional minute. Remove from the heat and mix in the parsley, lemon zest and juice, and season with salt and pepper.

5. Divide the vegetable mixture evenly among the oysters and bake for 10 to 12 minutes until the vegetables are lightly browned.

Nutrition:
- Calories: 134;
- Total Fat: 7 g
- Protein: 6 g
- Carbohydrates: 11 g
- Sugars: 7 g
- Fiber: 2 g

39. Tropical Shrimp Cocktail

Preparation time: 15 minutes
Cooking time: 3 minutes
Servings: 4
Ingredients:
- 1 pound medium shrimp, peeled and deveined
- 1 cup diced mango
- 2 ripe avocados, diced
- 1/4 cup finely diced red onion
- 2 roma tomatoes, diced
- 1/4 cup chopped fresh cilantro
- 2 tablespoons Low-Carb No-Cook Tomato Ketchup (here)
- Juice of 1 lime
- Juice of 1 orange
- 1 tablespoon extra-virgin olive oil
- 1 jalapeño pepper, seeded and minced
- Lime wedges, for serving

Directions:
1. Fill a large pot about halfway with water and bring to a boil. Meanwhile, fill a large bowl 2/3 of the way with ice and about 1 cup of cold water.
2. Add the shrimp to the boiling water and cook for 3 minutes until they are opaque and firm. Drain and quickly transfer to the ice water bath for 3 minutes to stop the cooking and cool them. Drain and pat the shrimp dry with a clean paper towel.
3. In a large bowl, mix together the shrimp, mango, avocado, red onion, tomatoes, and cilantro.
4. In a small bowl, combine the ketchup, lime juice, orange juice, oil, and jalapeño. Mix well and gently fold the sauce into the shrimp mixture.
5. Divide among 4 glasses or small dishes, with a lime wedge on the rim of each.

Nutrition:
- Calories: 279;
- Total Fat: 16 g
- Protein: 18 g
- Carbohydrates: 20 g
- Sugars: 10 g
- Fiber: 6 g

40. Pork Chop Diane

Preparation time: 10 minutes
Cooking time: 20 minutes
Servings: 4
Ingredients:
- 1/4 cup low-sodium chicken broth
- 1 tablespoon freshly squeezed lemon juice
- 2 teaspoons Worcestershire sauce
- 2 teaspoons Dijon mustard
- 4 (5-ounce) boneless pork top loin chops
- 1 teaspoon extra-virgin olive oil
- 1 teaspoon lemon zest
- 1 teaspoon butter
- 2 teaspoons chopped fresh chives

Directions:
1. Blend together the chicken broth, lemon juice, Worcestershire sauce, and Dijon mustard and set it aside.
2. Season the pork chops lightly.
3. Situate large skillet over medium-high heat and add the olive oil.
4. Cook the pork chops, turning once, until they are no longer pink, about 8 minutes per side.
5. Put aside the chops.
6. Pour the broth mixture into the skillet and cook until warmed through and thickened, about 2 minutes.
7. Blend lemon zest, butter, and chives.
8. Garnish with a generous spoonful of sauce.

Nutrition:
- Calories 200
- Fat 8 g
- Carbohydrates 1 g

41. Chipotle Chili Pork Chops

Preparation time: 4 hours
Cooking time: 20 minutes
Servings: 4
Ingredients:
- Juice and zest of 1 lime
- 1 tablespoon extra-virgin olive oil
- 1 tablespoon chipotle chili powder
- 2 teaspoons minced garlic
- 1 teaspoon ground cinnamon
- Pinch sea salt
- 4 (5-ounce) pork chops

Directions:
1. Combine the lime juice and zest, oil, chipotle chili powder, garlic, cinnamon, and salt in a resealable plastic bag. Add the pork chops. Remove as much air as possible and seal the bag.
2. Marinate the chops in the refrigerator for at least 4 hours, and up to 24 hours, turning them several times.
3. Ready the oven to 400°F and set a rack on a baking sheet. Let the chops rest at room temperature for 15 minutes, then arrange them on the rack and discard the remaining marinade.
4. Roast the chops until cooked through, turning once, about 10 minutes per side.
5. Serve with lime wedges.

Nutrition:
- Calories 204
- Carbohydrates 1 g
- Sugar 1 g

42. Orange-Marinated Pork Tenderloin

Preparation time: 2 hours
Cooking time: 30 minutes
Servings: 4
Ingredients:
- 1/4 cup freshly squeezed orange juice
- 2 teaspoons orange zest
- 2 teaspoons minced garlic
- 1 teaspoon low-sodium soy sauce
- 1 teaspoon grated fresh ginger
- 1 teaspoon honey
- 1 1/2 pounds pork tenderloin roast
- 1 tablespoon extra-virgin olive oil

Directions:
1. Blend together the orange juice, zest, garlic, soy sauce, ginger, and honey.
2. Pour the marinade into a resealable plastic bag and add the pork tenderloin.
3. Remove as much air as possible and seal the bag. Marinate the pork in the refrigerator, turning the bag a few times, for 2 hours.
4. Preheat the oven to 400°F.
5. Pull out tenderloin from the marinade and discard the marinade.
6. Position big ovenproof skillet over medium-high heat and add the oil.
7. Sear the pork tenderloin on all sides, about 5 minutes in total.
8. Position skillet to the oven and roast for 25 minutes.
9. Put aside for 10 minutes before serving.

Nutrition:
- Calories 228
- Carbohydrates 4 g
- Sugar 3 g

43. Homestyle Herb Meatballs

Preparation time: 10 minutes
Cooking time: 15 minutes
Servings: 4
Ingredients:
- 1/2 pound lean ground pork
- 1/2 pound lean ground beef
- 1 sweet onion, finely chopped
- 1/4 cup bread crumbs
- 2 tablespoons chopped fresh basil
- 2 teaspoons minced garlic
- 1 egg

Directions:
1. Preheat the oven to 350°F.
2. Ready baking tray with parchment paper and set it aside.
3. In a large bowl, mix together the pork, beef, onion, bread crumbs, basil, garlic, egg salt, and pepper until very well mixed.
4. Roll the meat mixture into 2-inch meatballs.
5. Transfer the meatballs to the baking sheet and bake until they are browned and cooked through, about 15 minutes.

6. Serve the meatballs with your favorite marinara sauce and some steamed green beans.

Nutrition:
- Calories 332
- Carbohydrates 13 g
- Sugar 3 g

44. Lime-Parsley Lamb Cutlets

Preparation time: 4 hours
Cooking time: 10 minutes
Servings: 4
Ingredients:
- 1/4 cup extra-virgin olive oil
- 1/4 cup freshly squeezed lime juice
- 2 tablespoons lime zest
- 2 tablespoons chopped fresh parsley
- 12 lamb cutlets (about 1 ½ pound total)

Directions:
1. Scourge the oil, lime juice, zest, parsley, salt, and pepper.
2. Pour marinade into a resealable plastic bag.
3. Add the cutlets to the bag and remove as much air as possible before sealing.
4. Marinate the lamb in the refrigerator for about 4 hours, turning the bag several times.
5. Preheat the oven to broil.
6. Remove the chops from the bag and arrange them on an aluminum foil–lined baking sheet. Discard the marinade.
7. Broil the chops for 4 minutes per side for medium doneness.
8. Let the chops rest for 5 minutes before serving.

Nutrition:
- Calories 413
- Carbohydrates 1 g
- Protein 31 g

45. Mediterranean Steak Sandwiches

Preparation time: 1 hour
Cooking time: 10 minutes
Servings: 4
Ingredients:
- 2 tablespoons extra-virgin olive oil
- 2 tablespoons balsamic vinegar
- 2 teaspoons garlic
- 2 teaspoons lemon juice
- 2 teaspoons fresh oregano
- 1 teaspoon fresh parsley
- 1-pound flank steak
- 4 whole-wheat pitas
- 2 cups shredded lettuce
- 1 red onion, thinly sliced
- 1 tomato, chopped
- 1 ounce low-sodium feta cheese

Directions:
1. Scourge olive oil, balsamic vinegar, garlic, lemon juice, oregano, and parsley.
2. Add the steak to the bowl, turning to coat it completely.
3. Marinate the steak for 1 hour in the refrigerator, turning it over several times.
4. Preheat the broiler. Line a baking sheet with aluminum foil.
5. Put steak out of the bowl and discard the marinade.
6. Situate steak on the baking sheet and broil for 5 minutes per side for medium.
7. Set aside for 10 minutes before slicing.
8. Stuff the pitas with the sliced steak, lettuce, onion, tomato, and feta.

Nutrition:
- Calories 344
- Carbohydrates 22 g
- Fiber 3 g

46. Roasted Beef with Peppercorn Sauce

Preparation time: 10 minutes
Cooking time: 90 minutes
Servings: 4
Ingredients:
- 1 ½ pound top rump beef roast
- 3 teaspoons extra-virgin olive oil
- 3 shallots, minced
- 2 teaspoons minced garlic
- 1 tablespoon green peppercorns
- 2 tablespoons dry sherry
- 2 tablespoons all-purpose flour
- 1 cup sodium-free beef broth

Directions:
1. Heat the oven to 300°F.
2. Season the roast with salt and pepper.
3. Position a huge skillet over medium-high heat and add 2 teaspoons of olive oil.

4. Brown the beef on all sides, about 10 minutes in total, and transfer the roast to a baking dish.
5. Roast until desired doneness, about 1 ½ hour for medium. When the roast has been in the oven for 1 hour, start the sauce.
6. In a medium saucepan over medium-high heat, sauté the shallots in the remaining 1 teaspoon of olive oil until translucent, about 4 minutes.
7. Stir in the garlic and peppercorns, and cook for another minute. Whisk in the sherry to deglaze the pan.
8. Whisk in the flour to form a thick paste, cooking for 1 minute and stirring constantly.
9. Fill in the beef broth and whisk for 4 minutes. Season the sauce.
10. Serve the beef with a generous spoonful of sauce.

Nutrition:
- Calories 330
- Carbohydrates 4 g
- Protein 36 g

47. Coffee-and-Herb-Marinated Steak

Preparation time: 2 hours
Cooking time: 10 minutes
Servings: 3
Ingredients:
- 1/4 cup whole coffee beans
- 2 teaspoons garlic
- 2 teaspoons rosemary
- 2 teaspoons thyme
- 1 teaspoon black pepper
- 2 tablespoons apple cider vinegar
- 2 tablespoons extra-virgin olive oil
- 1-pound flank steak, trimmed of visible fat

Directions:
1. Place the coffee beans, garlic, rosemary, thyme, and black pepper in a coffee grinder or food processor and pulse until coarsely ground.
2. Transfer the coffee mixture to a resealable plastic bag and add the vinegar and oil. Shake to combine.
3. Add the flank steak and squeeze the excess air out of the bag. Seal it. Marinate the steak in the refrigerator for at least 2 hours, occasionally turning the bag over.
4. Preheat the broiler. Line a baking sheet with aluminum foil.
5. Pull the steak out and discard the marinade.
6. Position steak on the baking sheet and broil until it is done to your liking.
7. Put aside for 10 minutes before cutting it.
8. Serve with your favorite side dish.

Nutrition:
- Calories 313 Fat 20 g Protein 31 g

48. Traditional Beef Stroganoff

Preparation time: 10 minutes
Cooking time: 30 minutes
Servings: 4
Ingredients:
- 1 teaspoon extra-virgin olive oil
- 1-pound top sirloin, cut into thin strips
- 1 cup sliced button mushrooms
- 1/2 sweet onion, finely chopped
- 1 teaspoon minced garlic
- 1 tablespoon whole-wheat flour
- 1/2 cup low-sodium beef broth
- 1/4 cup dry sherry
- 1/2 cup fat-free sour cream
- 1 tablespoon chopped fresh parsley

Directions:
1. Position the skillet over medium-high heat and add the oil.
2. Sauté the beef until browned, about 10 minutes, then remove the beef with a slotted spoon to a plate and set it aside.
3. Add the mushrooms, onion, and garlic to the skillet and sauté until lightly browned, about 5 minutes.
4. Whisk in the flour and then whisk in the beef broth and sherry.
5. Return the sirloin to the skillet and bring the mixture to a boil.
6. Reduce the heat to low and simmer until the beef is tender, about 10 minutes.
7. Stir in the sour cream and parsley. Season with salt and pepper.

Nutrition:
- Calories 257
- Carbohydrates 6 g
- Fiber 1 g

49. Pork Chops with Grape Sauce

Preparation time: 15 minutes
Cooking time: 25 minutes
Servings: 4
Ingredients:
- Cooking spray
- 4 pork chops
- 1/4 cup onion, sliced
- 1 clove garlic, minced
- 1/2 cup low-sodium chicken broth
- 3/4 cup apple juice
- 1 tablespoon cornstarch
- 1 tablespoon balsamic vinegar
- 1 teaspoon honey
- 1 cup seedless red grapes, sliced in half

Directions:
1. Spray oil on your pan.
2. Put it over medium heat.
3. Add the pork chops to the pan.
4. Cook for 5 minutes per side.
5. Remove and set aside.
6. Add onion and garlic.
7. Cook for 2 minutes.
8. Pour in the broth and apple juice.
9. Bring to a boil.
10. Reduce heat to simmer.
11. Put the pork chops back to the skillet.
12. Simmer for 4 minutes.
13. In a bowl, mix the cornstarch, vinegar and honey.
14. Add to the pan.
15. Cook until the sauce has thickened.
16. Add the grapes.
17. Pour sauce over the pork chops before serving.

Nutrition:
- Calories 188;
- Total Fat 4 g
- Saturated Fat 1 g
- Cholesterol 47 mg
- Sodium 117 mg
- Total Carbohydrate 18 g
- Dietary Fiber 1 g
- Total Sugars 13 g
- Protein 19 g
- Potassium 759 mg

50. Roasted Pork & Apples

Preparation time: 15 minutes
Cooking time: 30 minutes
Servings: 4
Ingredients:
- Salt and pepper to taste
- 1/2 teaspoon dried, crushed
- 1 lb. pork tenderloin
- 1 tablespoon canola oil
- 1 onion, sliced into wedges
- 3 cooking apples, sliced into wedges
- 2/3 cup apple cider
- Sprigs fresh sage

Directions:
1. In a bowl, mix salt, pepper and sage.
2. Season both sides of pork with this mixture.
3. Place a pan over medium heat.
4. Brown both sides.
5. Transfer to a roasting pan.
6. Add the onion on top and around the pork.
7. Drizzle oil on top of the pork and apples.
8. Roast in the oven at 425 degrees F for 10 minutes.
9. Add the apples, roast for another 15 minutes.
10. In a pan, boil the apple cider and then simmer for 10 minutes.
11. Pour the apple cider sauce over the pork before serving.

Nutrition:
- Calories 239;
- Total Fat 6 g
- Saturated Fat 1 g
- Cholesterol 74 mg
- Sodium 209 mg
- Total Carbohydrate 22 g
- Dietary Fiber 3 g
- Total Sugars 16 g
- Protein 24 g
- Potassium 655 mg

51. Pork with Cranberry Relish

Preparation time: 30 minutes
Cooking time: 30 minutes
Servings: 4
Ingredients:
- 12 oz. pork tenderloin, fat trimmed and sliced crosswise
- Salt and pepper to taste

- 1/4 cup all-purpose flour
- 2 tablespoons olive oil
- 1 onion, sliced thinly
- 1/4 cup dried cranberries
- 1/4 cup low-sodium chicken broth
- 1 tablespoon balsamic vinegar

Directions:
1. Flatten each slice of pork using a mallet.
2. In a dish, mix the salt, pepper and flour.
3. Dip each pork slice into the flour mixture.
4. Add oil to a pan over medium-high heat.
5. Cook pork for 3 minutes per side or until golden crispy.
6. Transfer to a serving plate and cover with foil.
7. Cook the onion in the pan for 4 minutes.
8. Stir in the rest of the ingredients.
9. Simmer until the sauce has thickened.

Nutrition:
- Calories 211;
- Total Fat 9 g
- Saturated Fat 2 g
- Cholesterol 53 mg
- Sodium 116 mg
- Total Carbohydrate 15 g
- Dietary Fiber 1 g
- Total Sugars 6 g
- Protein 18 g
- Potassium 378 mg

52. Sesame Pork with Mustard Sauce

Preparation time: 25 minutes
Cooking time: 25 minutes
Servings: 4
Ingredients:
- 2 tablespoons low-sodium teriyaki sauce
- 1/4 cup chili sauce
- 2 cloves garlic, minced
- 2 teaspoons ginger, grated
- 2 pork tenderloins
- 2 teaspoons sesame seeds
- 1/4 cup low fat sour cream
- 1 teaspoon Dijon mustard
- Salt to taste
- 1 scallion, chopped

Directions:
1. Preheat your oven to 425 degrees F.
2. Mix the teriyaki sauce, chili sauce, garlic and ginger.
3. Put the pork on a roasting pan.
4. Brush the sauce on both sides of the pork.
5. Bake in the oven for 15 minutes.
6. Brush with more sauce.
7. Top with sesame seeds.
8. Roast for 10 more minutes.
9. Mix the rest of the ingredients.
10. Serve the pork with mustard sauce.

Nutrition:
- Calories 135;
- Total Fat 3 g
- Saturated Fat 1 g
- Cholesterol 56 mg
- Sodium 302 mg
- Total Carbohydrate 7 g
- Dietary Fiber 1 g
- Total Sugars 15 g
- Protein 20 g
- Potassium 755 mg

53. Steak with Mushroom Sauce

Preparation time: 20 minutes
Cooking time: 5 minutes
Servings: 4
Ingredients:
- 12 oz. sirloin steak, sliced and trimmed
- 2 teaspoons grilling seasoning
- 2 teaspoons oil
- 6 oz. broccoli, trimmed
- 2 cups frozen peas
- 3 cups fresh mushrooms, sliced
- 1 cup beef broth (unsalted)
- 1 tablespoon mustard
- 2 teaspoons cornstarch
- Salt to taste

Directions:
1. Preheat your oven to 350 degrees F.
2. Season meat with grilling seasoning.
3. In a pan over medium-high heat, cook the meat and broccoli for 4 minutes.
4. Sprinkle the peas around the steak.
5. Put the pan inside the oven and bake for 8 minutes.

6. Remove both meat and vegetables from the pan.
7. Add the mushrooms to the pan.
8. Cook for 3 minutes.
9. Mix the broth, mustard, salt and cornstarch.
10. Add to the mushrooms.
11. Cook for 1 minute.
12. Pour sauce over meat and vegetables before serving.

Nutrition:
- Calories 226; Total Fat 6;
- Saturated Fat 2 g Cholesterol 51 mg
- Sodium 356 mg Total Carbohydrate 16 g
- Dietary Fiber 5 g Total Sugars 6 g
- Protein 26 g Potassium 780 mg

54. Steak with Tomato & Herbs

Preparation time: 30 minutes
Cooking time: 30 minutes
Servings: 2
Ingredients:
- 8 oz. beef loin steak, sliced in half
- Salt and pepper to taste
- Cooking spray
- 1 teaspoon fresh basil, snipped
- 1/4 cup green onion, sliced
- 1/2 cup tomato, chopped

Directions:
1. Season the steak with salt and pepper.
2. Spray oil on your pan.
3. Put the pan over medium-high heat.
4. Once hot, add the steaks.
5. Reduce heat to medium.
6. Cook for 10 to 13 minutes for medium, turning once.
7. Add the basil and green onion.
8. Cook for 2 minutes.
9. Add the tomato.
10. Cook for 1 minute.
11. Let cool a little before slicing.

Nutrition:
- Calories 170; Total Fat 6 g
- Saturated Fat 2 g Cholesterol 66 mg
- Sodium 207 mg Total Carbohydrate 3 g
- Dietary Fiber 1 g
- Total Sugars 5 g
- Protein 25 g
- Potassium 477 mg

55. Beef & Asparagus

Preparation time: 15 minutes
Cooking time: 10 minutes
Servings: 4
Ingredients:
- 2 teaspoons olive oil
- 1 lb. lean beef sirloin, trimmed and sliced
- 1 carrot, shredded
- Salt and pepper to taste
- 12 oz. asparagus, trimmed and sliced
- 1 teaspoon dried herbs de Provence, crushed
- 1/2 cup Marsala
- 1/4 teaspoon lemon zest

Directions:
1. Pour oil in a pan over medium heat.
2. Add the beef and carrot.
3. Season with salt and pepper.
4. Cook for 3 minutes.
5. Add the asparagus and herbs.
6. Cook for 2 minutes.
7. Add the Marsala and lemon zest.
8. Cook for 5 minutes, stirring frequently.

Nutrition:
- Calories 327;
- Total Fat 7 g
- Saturated Fat 2 g
- Cholesterol 69 mg
- Sodium 209 mg
- Total Carbohydrate 29 g
- Dietary Fiber 2 g
- Total Sugars 3 g
- Protein 28 g
- Potassium 576 mg

56. Italian Beef

Preparation time: 20 minutes
Cooking time: 1 hour and 20 minutes
Servings: 4
Ingredients:
- Cooking spray
- 1 lb. beef round steak, trimmed and sliced
- 1 cup onion, chopped
- 2 cloves garlic, minced
- 1 cup green bell pepper, chopped
- 1/2 cup celery, chopped
- 2 cups mushrooms, sliced
- 14 1/2 oz. canned diced tomatoes

- 1/2 teaspoon dried basil
- 1/4 teaspoon dried oregano
- 1/8 teaspoon crushed red pepper
- 2 tablespoons Parmesan cheese, grated

Directions:
1. Spray oil on the pan over medium heat.
2. Cook the meat until brown on both sides.
3. Transfer meat to a plate.
4. Add the onion, garlic, bell pepper, celery and mushroom to the pan.
5. Cook until tender.
6. Add the tomatoes, herbs, and pepper.
7. Put the meat back to the pan.
8. Simmer while covered for 1 hour and 15 minutes.
9. Stir occasionally.
10. Sprinkle Parmesan cheese on top of the dish before serving.

Nutrition:
- Calories 212;
- Total Fat 4 g
- Saturated Fat 1 g
- Cholesterol 51 mg
- Sodium 296 mg
- Total Sugars 6 g
- Protein 30 g
- Potassium 876 mg

57. Barbecue Beef Brisket

Preparation time: 25 Minutes
Cooking time: 10 hours
Servings: 10
Ingredients:
- 4 lb. beef brisket (boneless), trimmed and sliced
- 1 bay leaf
- 2 onions, sliced into rings
- 1/2 teaspoon dried thyme, crushed
- 1/4 cup chili sauce
- 1 clove garlic, minced
- Salt and pepper to taste
- 2 tablespoons light brown sugar
- 2 tablespoons cornstarch
- 2 tablespoons cold water

Directions:
1. Put the meat in a slow cooker.
2. Add the bay leaf and onion.
3. In a bowl, mix the thyme, chili sauce, salt, pepper and sugar.
4. Pour the sauce over the meat.
5. Mix well.
6. Seal the pot and cook on low heat for 10 hours.
7. Discard the bay leaf.
8. Pour cooking liquid in a pan.
9. Add the mixed water and cornstarch.
10. Simmer until the sauce has thickened.
11. Pour the sauce over the meat.

Nutrition:
- Calories 182;
- Total Fat 6 g
- Saturated Fat 2 g
- Cholesterol 57 mg
- Sodium 217 mg
- Total Sugars 4 g
- Protein 20 g
- Potassium 383 mg

58. Lamb with Broccoli & Carrots

Preparation time: 20 minutes
Cooking time: 10 minutes
Servings: 4
Ingredients:
- 2 cloves garlic, minced
- 1 tablespoon fresh ginger, grated
- 1/4 teaspoon red pepper, crushed
- 2 tablespoons low-sodium soy sauce
- 1 tablespoon white vinegar
- 1 tablespoon cornstarch
- 12 oz. lamb meat, trimmed and sliced
- 2 teaspoons cooking oil
- 1 lb. broccoli, sliced into florets
- 2 carrots, sliced into strips
- 3/4 cup low-sodium beef broth
- 4 green onions, chopped
- 2 cups cooked spaghetti squash pasta

Directions:
1. Combine the garlic, ginger, red pepper, soy sauce, vinegar and cornstarch in a bowl.
2. Add lamb to the marinade.
3. Marinate for 10 minutes.
4. Discard marinade.
5. In a pan over medium heat, add the oil.
6. Add the lamb and cook for 3 minutes.
7. Transfer lamb to a plate.

8. Add the broccoli and carrots.
9. Cook for 1 minute.
10. Pour in the beef broth.
11. Cook for 5 minutes.
12. Put the meat back to the pan.
13. Sprinkle with green onion and serve on top of spaghetti squash.

Nutrition:
- Calories 205;
- Total Fat 6 g
- Saturated Fat 1 g
- Cholesterol 40 mg
- Sodium 659 mg
- Total Carb. 17 g

59. Beef Chili

Preparation time: 10 Minutes
Cooking time: 20 Minutes
Servings: 4
Ingredients:
- 1/2 tsp. Garlic Powder
- 1 tsp. Coriander, grounded
- 1 lb. Beef, grounded
- 1/2 tsp. Sea Salt
- 1/2 tsp. Cayenne Pepper
- 1 tsp. Cumin, grounded
- 1/2 tsp. Pepper, grounded
- 1/2 cup Salsa, low-carb & no-sugar

Directions:
1. Heat a large-sized pan over medium-high heat and cook the beef in it until browned.
2. Stir in all the spices and cook them for 7 minutes or until everything is combined.
3. When the beef gets cooked, spoon in the salsa.
4. Bring the mixture to a simmer and cook for another 8 minutes or until everything comes together.
5. Take it from heat and transfer to a serving bowl.

Nutrition:
- Calories: 229
- Fat: 10 g
- Carbohydrates: 2 g
- Proteins: 33 g
- Sodium: 675 mg

CHAPTER 7:

Dinner Recipes

60. Wholesome Broccoli Pork Chops

Cooking time: 10 minutes
Preparation time: 10–15 minutes
Servings: 4
Ingredients:

- 1 1/2 tablespoons canola oil (divided)
- 1/4 teaspoon red pepper flakes, crushed
- 1 clove garlic, minced
- 1 pound pork loin chops, boneless and divided into 4 equal parts
- 2 cups broccoli florets
- 2 tablespoons + 1 teaspoon reduced-sodium soy sauce
- 2 tablespoons water
- 3 tablespoons rice wine vinegar
- 2 tablespoons cilantro, chopped

Directions:

1. Add the water, soy sauce, vinegar, red pepper, garlic, and 1 tablespoon of the canola oil to a mixing bowl. Mix well.
2. Add the pork chops and combine well.
3. Refrigerate for 20-30 minutes to marinate.
4. Steam the broccoli florets over boiling water for 5 minutes; drain and set aside.
5. Heat the remaining 1/2 tablespoon of canola oil over medium heat in a medium saucepan or skillet.
6. Add the pork chops (reserve the marinade) and stir-cook for 4-5 minutes until evenly brown. Transfer the chops to a serving platter.
7. In another saucepan, boil the reserved marinade.
8. Cover and simmer the mixture over low heat for about 2-3 minutes until it thickens.
9. Pour it over the pork chops; top with chopped cilantro and serve with cooked broccoli on the side.

Nutrition:

- Calories 235,
- Fat 13 g
- Total carbs 5 g
- Sugar 1 g
- Protein 23 g
- Sodium 480 mg

61. Lemony Dijon Meat Loaf

Preparation time: 10 minutes
Cooking time: 35 minutes
Servings: 3-4
Ingredients:

- 2 pounds lean ground beef
- 1 cup almond meal
- 2 eggs
- 1 tablespoon lemon, zest, and juice
- 2 teaspoons Dijon mustard
- Seasoning Salt and black pepper, to taste

Directions:

1. Pour 1-1/2 cups of water and place trivet inside the instant pot.
2. Mix all the listed ingredients in a mixing bowl. Make a large loaf of the meat mixture.
3. Now place meatloaf over an aluminum foil and wrap the meat in foil.
4. Place foil on the trivet.
5. Lock the lid of the instant Pot and set a timer to 35 minutes at high pressure.
6. Once timer beeps, do a natural release for 15 minutes, followed by quick release.
7. Remove the meatloaf from the foil.
8. Transfer to cutting board, and cut into slices after letting it get cold. Serve.

Nutrition:

- Calories: 559
- Protein: 65.25 g
- Fat: 30.26 g
- Carbohydrates: 2.05 g

62. Italian Pork Chops

Preparation time: 5 minutes
Cooking time: 25 minutes
Servings: 4
Ingredients:

- 4 cloves garlic, sliced
- 4 thick pork chops, fat trimmed
- 1 small yellow onion, cut into rings
- 1/2 cup low-fat mozzarella cheese
- 1 (28-ounce) can diced tomatoes
- 1 teaspoon paprika
- 1 teaspoon dried oregano
- 1 chicken bouillon cube
- Salt and pepper to taste

Directions:
1. Preheat the oven to 400°F (200°C). Grease a baking pan with some cooking spray.
2. Season the pork chops with pepper.
3. Grease a medium saucepan or skillet with cooking spray and heat it over medium heat.
4. Add the pork chops and stir-cook for 2 minutes per side until evenly brown.
5. Add the garlic and onion rings and stir-cook for 1-2 minutes until softened.
6. Add the spices, tomato and bouillon cube; simmer for 2-3 minutes.
7. Pour in the tomato sauce.
8. Add the mixture to the baking pan, top with the cheese, and bake for about 20 minutes until the top is golden brown.
9. Let cool slightly and serve warm.

Note: You can store leftovers in an airtight container in the refrigerator for up to 3-4 days. Simply reheat in a saucepan and serve.

Nutrition:
- Calories 405
- Fat 17 g
- Total carbs 16 g
- Sugar 7.5 g
- Protein 43.5 g
- Sodium 1275 mg

63. Tomato Steak Kebabs

Preparation time: 10-15 minutes
Cooking time: 10 minutes
Servings: 4
Ingredients:
- 1 teaspoon Dijon mustard
- 1 pound top sirloin steak, cut into 1-inch cubes
- 1/4 cup balsamic vinaigrette
- 2 cups cherry tomatoes
- 1/4 cup barbecue sauce

Directions:
1. Add the barbecue sauce, vinaigrette and mustard to a mixing bowl; mix well. Set aside 1/4 of the mixture.
2. Add the beef and coat well.
3. Take four metal or soaked wooden skewers and thread them alternately with tomatoes and beef pieces.
4. Preheat the grill to medium-high heat. Grease the grill rack with cooking spray.
5. Grill the skewers for 6-8 minutes until the beef is tender. When 3-4 minutes remain, begin basting frequently with the reserved mixture.

Nutrition:
- Calories 194, Fat 7 g
- Total carbs 7 g Sugar 5 g Protein 25 g
- Sodium 288 mg

64. Pork Mushroom Stew

Preparation time: 10 minutes
Cooking time: 90 minutes
Servings: 4
Ingredients:
- 1 (16-ounce) can unsalted tomato sauce
- 2 cups carrots, sliced
- 1 medium green pepper, chopped
- 1/2 pound mushrooms, sliced
- 1 teaspoon dried basil
- 1/2 teaspoon dried rosemary, crushed
- 1 pound lean boneless pork, cut into 1-inch cubes
- 1 cup onion, chopped
- 1/2 cup water
- 1/4 teaspoon pepper

Directions:
1. Grease a large cooking pot or Dutch oven with some cooking oil and heat it over medium heat.
2. Add the pork and stir-cook to brown evenly.
3. Add the onion, seasonings, water and tomato sauce; stir.
4. Bring to a boil, cover, and simmer over low heat for about 60 minutes until the pork is tender.
5. Add the other ingredients; combine and cook for 30 more minutes until the veggies are tender.
6. Serve warm.

Nutrition:
- Calories 201 Fat 7 g
- Total carbs 15 g Sugar 0 g
- Protein 18 g
- Sodium 644 mg

65. Beef Steaks with Green Asparagus

Preparation time: 15 minutes
Cooking time: 20 minutes
Servings: 4
Ingredients:
- 500 g asparagus, green
- 40 g herb butter
- 2 beef fillet steaks (approx. 150 g each)
- 1 dried tomato pickled in oil
- 50 g ricotta
- Sea salt and black pepper
- Herbs, fresh e.g., B. oregano, basil
- 1 tbsp. oil for frying & capers, as desired (optional)

Directions:
1. Wash the asparagus and peel the lower ends. Prepare two pieces of baking paper or aluminum foil and spread the asparagus on top. Put the herb butter on the asparagus, close the foil tightly, put on the grill for about 10 - 15 minutes.
2. Dab steaks with a little paper towel, cut a pocket. Drain the tomatoes and cut into small pieces. Put the ricotta and capers in a bowl, wash, dry and chop the herbs and add them as well.
3. Mix everything well and season with sea salt and pepper. Pour the finished cream into the steaks and seal the openings with a toothpick.
4. Finally, season the steaks with sea salt and pepper, brush with the oil and grill depending on the degree of cooking required (approx. 5–8 minutes on each side).
5. Arrange the steaks with the asparagus, add the rest of the cream and serve hot.

Note: If you don't have a grill, you can prepare both the asparagus and the steaks in the oven. First fry the steaks briefly in the pan and then finish cooking in the oven.

Nutrition:
- Calories: 339
- Protein: 18.91 g
- Fat: 27.06 g
- Carbohydrates: 6.31 g

66. Garlic Chicken Balls

Preparation time: 15 minutes
Cooking time: 10 minutes
Servings: 4
Ingredients:
- 2 cups ground chicken
- 1 teaspoon minced garlic
- 1 teaspoon dried dill
- 1/3 carrot, grated
- 1 egg beaten
- 1 tablespoon olive oil
- 1/4 cup coconut flakes
- 1/2 teaspoon salt

Directions:
1. In the mixing bowl, mix up together ground chicken, minced garlic, dried dill, carrot, egg and salt.
2. Stir the chicken mixture with the assistance of the fingertips until homogeneous.
3. Then, make medium balls from the mixture.
4. Coat every chicken ball in coconut flakes.
5. Heat vegetable oil in the skillet.
6. Add chicken balls and cook them for 3 minutes from all sides. The cooked chicken balls will have a golden-brown color.

Nutrition:
- Calories 200
- Fat 11.5
- Fiber 0.6
- Carbs 1.7
- Protein 21.9

67. Mu Shu Lunch Pork

Preparation time: 5 minutes
Cooking time: 10 minutes
Servings: 2
Ingredients:
- 4 cups coleslaw mix, with carrots
- 1 small onion, sliced thin
- 1 lb. cooked roast pork, cut into 1/2 cubes
- 2 tablespoon hoisin sauce
- 2 tablespoon soy sauce

Directions:
1. In a large skillet, heat the oil on high heat.
2. Stir-fry the cabbage and onion for 4 minutes until tender.
3. Add the pork, hoisin, and soy.
4. Cook until browned. Enjoy!

Nutrition:
- Calories: 388
- Carbohydrates: 16 g
- Fat: 21 g
- Protein: 25 g
- Fiber: 16 g

68. Bacon & Chicken Patties

Preparation time: 5 minutes
Cooking time: 15 minutes
Servings: 2
Ingredients:
- 1 1/2 oz. can chicken breast
- 4 slices bacon
- 1/4 cup parmesan cheese
- 1 large egg
- 3 tablespoon flour

Directions:
1. Cook the bacon until crispy.
2. Chop the chicken and bacon together in a food processor until fine.
3. Add in the parmesan, egg flour, and blend.
4. Make the patties by hand and fry on medium heat in a pan with some oil.
5. Once browned, flip over, continue cooking and lay them to empty. Serve!

Nutrition:
- Calories: 387
- Carbohydrates: 13 g
- Fat: 16 g
- Protein: 34 g
- Fiber: 28 g

69. Autumn Pork Chops with Red Cabbage and Apples

Preparation time: 15 minutes
Cooking time: 30 minutes
Servings: 2
Ingredients:
- 1/8 Cup apple cider vinegar
- 1 tablespoon granulated sweetener
- 2 (4 oz.) pork chops, about 1 inch thick
- 1/2 tablespoon extra-virgin olive oil
- 1/4 red cabbage, finely shredded
- 1/2 sweet onion, thinly sliced
- 1/2 apple, peeled, cored, and sliced
- 1/2 teaspoon chopped fresh thyme

Directions:
1. Scourge together the vinegar and sweetener. Set it aside.
2. Season the pork with salt and pepper.
3. Position a big skillet over medium-high heat and add the olive oil.
4. Cook the pork chops until no longer pink, turning once, about 8 minutes per side.
5. Put chops aside.
6. Add the cabbage and onion to the skillet and sauté until the vegetables have softened about 5 minutes.
7. Add the vinegar mixture and the apple slices to the skillet and bring the mixture to boiling point.
8. Adjust low-heat and simmer for 5 additional minutes.
9. Return the pork chops to the skillet, along with any accumulated juices and thyme, cover, and cook for 5 more minutes.

Nutrition:
- Calories: 223
- Fat: 12 g
- Carbohydrates: 3 g

70. Creole Braised Sirloin

Preparation time: 15 minutes
Cooking time: 40 minutes
Servings: 4
Ingredients:
- 1 pound beef round sirloin tip, cut into 4 strips
- 1/4 tsp. freshly ground black pepper
- 2 cups chicken broth (here) or store-bought low-sodium chicken broth, divided
- 1 medium onion, chopped
- 1 celery stalk, coarsely chopped
- 1 medium green bell pepper, coarsely chopped

- 2 garlic cloves, minced
- 4 medium tomatoes, coarsely chopped
- 1 bunch mustard greens including stems, coarsely chopped
- 1 tbsp. creole seasoning
- 1/4 tsp. red pepper flakes
- 2 bay leaves

Directions:
1. Preheat the oven to 450°F.
2. Massage the beef all over with black pepper.
3. In a Dutch oven, bring 1 cup of broth to a simmer over medium heat.
4. Add the onion, celery, bell pepper, and garlic and cook, stirring often, for 5 minutes, or until the vegetables are softened.
5. Add the tomatoes, mustard greens, Creole seasoning and red pepper flakes and cook for 3 to 5 minutes, or until the greens are wilted.
6. Add the bay leaves, beef, and remaining 1 cup of broth.
7. Cover the pot, transfer to the oven, and cook for 30 minutes or until the juices run clear when you pierce the beef.
8. Remove the beef from the oven and let rest for 5 to 7 minutes. Discard the bay leaves.
9. Thinly slice the beef and serve.

Nutrition:
- Calories: 202
- Total fat: 5 g
- Cholesterol: 60 mg
- Sodium: 129 mg
- Total Carbohydrates: 14 g
- Protein: 28 g

71. Crispy Chicken Wings

Preparation time: 10 minutes
Cooking time: 20 minutes
Servings: 4
Ingredients:
- 1 tbsp. gluten-free baking powder
- 3/4 tsp. sea salt
- 2 lbs. chicken wings
- 1/4 tsp. black pepper

Directions:
1. Preheat the Air Fryer to 370°F. Merge the chicken wings, baking powder, sea salt, and black pepper.
2. Pour some grease on the Air Fryer basket. Arrange the wings in batches into the Air Fryer basket and cook at 250°F for 15 minutes.
3. Shake the Air Fryer or turn the wings to the other side and cook for another 15 minutes for the wings to be well cooked.
4. Serve.

Nutrition:
- Calories: 275
- Carbohydrates: 9 g
- Fat: 17 g
- Protein: 13 g

72. Herb Butter Lamb Chops

Preparation time: 10 minutes
Cooking time: 5 minutes
Servings: 4
Ingredients:
- 4 lamb chops
- 1 tsp. rosemary, chopped
- 1 tbsp. butter
- Pepper
- Salt

Directions:
1. Season lamb chops with pepper and salt.
2. Place the dehydrating tray in a multi-level air fryer basket and place the basket in the instant pot.
3. Place lamb chops on dehydrating tray.
4. Seal pot with air fryer lid and select air fry mode, then set the temperature to 400°F and timer for 5 minutes.
5. Mix together butter and rosemary and spread overcooked lamb chops.
6. Serve and enjoy.

Nutrition:
- Calories: 278 Fat: 12.8 g
- Carbohydrates: 0.2 g
- Sugar: 0 g
- Protein: 38 g
- Cholesterol: 129 mg

73. Rosemary Lemon Lamb Chops

Preparation time: 10 minutes
Cooking time: 6 minutes
Servings: 2
Ingredients:

- 2 lamb chops
- 1 tbsp. dried rosemary
- 2 tbsps. lemon juice

Directions:

1. Mix together rosemary and lemon juice and brush over lamb chops.
2. Place the dehydrating tray in a multi-level air fryer basket and place the basket in the instant pot.
3. Place lamb chops on dehydrating tray.
4. Seal pot with air fryer lid and select air fry mode, then set the temperature to 400°F and timer for 6 minutes. Turn lamb chops halfway through.
5. Serve and enjoy.

Nutrition:

- Calories: 260
- Fat: 10.3 g
- Carbohydrates: 1.4 g
- Protein: 38.1 g
- Cholesterol: 122 mg

74. Herb Garlic Lamb Chops

Preparation time: 10 minutes
Cooking time: 6 minutes
Servings: 3
Ingredients:

- 3 lamb loin chops
- 1 tbsp. lemon juice
- 1 tbsp. lemon zest, grated
- 2 tsps. dried rosemary
- 1 tsp. dried thyme
- 1 tbsp. olive oil
- 2 tsps. garlic, minced

Directions:

1. Mix together lemon juice, lemon zest, rosemary, thyme, oil, and garlic, and rub over lamb chops.
2. Place the dehydrating tray in a multi-level air fryer basket and place the basket in the instant pot.
3. Place lamb chops on dehydrating tray.
4. Seal pot with air fryer lid and select air fry mode, then set the temperature to 400°F and timer for 6 minutes. Turn lamb chops halfway through.
5. Serve and enjoy.

Nutrition:

- Calories: 300
- Fat: 14.8 g
- Carbohydrates: 1.9 g
- Sugar: 0.3 g
- Protein: 38.2 g
- Cholesterol: 122 mg

75. Delicious Lamb Chops

Preparation time: 10 minutes
Cooking time: 8 minutes
Servings: 4
Ingredients:

- 1 lb. lamb chops
- 2 tbsps. lemon juice
- 2 tbsps. olive oil
- 1 tsp. ground coriander
- 1 tsp. oregano
- 1 tsp. thyme
- 1 tsp. rosemary
- 1 tsp. salt

Directions:

1. Add lamb chops and remaining ingredients into the zip-lock bag. Shake well and place it in the refrigerator for 1 hour.
2. Place the dehydrating tray in a multi-level air fryer basket and place the basket in the instant pot.
3. Place lamb chops on dehydrating tray.
4. Seal pot with air fryer lid and select air fry mode, then set the temperature to 400°F and timer for 8 minutes. Turn lamb chops halfway through.
5. Serve and enjoy.

Nutrition:

- Calories: 276
- Fat: 15.5 g
- Carbohydrates: 0.8 g
- Sugar: 0.2 g
- Protein: 32 g
- Cholesterol: 102 mg

76. Pork Tenderloin with Bell Peppers

Preparation time: 20 minutes
Cooking time: 15 minutes
Servings: 3
Ingredients:
- 1 large red bell pepper, seeded and cut into thin strips
- 1 red onion, thinly sliced
- 2 tsps. Herbs de Provence
- Salt and ground black pepper, as required
- 1 tbsp. olive oil
- 10 1/2-oz pork tenderloin, cut into 4 pieces
- 1/2 tbsp. Dijon mustard

Directions:
1. In a bowl, add the bell pepper, onion, Herbs de Provence, salt, black pepper, and 1/2 tbsp. of oil and toss to coat well.
2. Rub the pork pieces with mustard, salt, and black pepper.
3. Drizzle with the remaining oil.
4. Set the temperature of the air fryer to 390°F. Grease an air fryer pan.
5. Place bell pepper mixture into the prepared Air Fryer pan and top with the pork pieces.
6. Air fry for about 15 minutes, flipping once halfway through.
7. Remove from air fryer and transfer the pork mixture onto serving plates.
8. Serve hot.

Nutrition:
- Calories: 218
- Carbohydrate: 7.1 g
- Protein: 27.7 g
- Fat: 8.8 g
- Sugar: 3.7 g

77. Pork Tenderloin with Bacon & Veggies

Preparation time: 20 minutes
Cooking time: 28 minutes
Servings: 3
Ingredients:
- 3 potatoes
- 3/4 pound frozen green beans
- 6 bacon slices
- 3 6-ounces pork tenderloins
- 2 tbsps. olive oil

Directions:
1. Set the temperature of the air fryer to 390°F. Grease an air fryer basket.
2. With a fork, pierce the potatoes.
3. Place potatoes into the prepared air fryer basket and air fry for about 15 minutes.
4. Wrap one bacon slice around 4-6 green beans.
5. Coat the pork tenderloins with oil.
6. After 15 minutes, add the pork tenderloins into the air fryer basket with potatoes and air fry for about 5-6 minutes.
7. Remove the pork tenderloins from the basket.
8. Place bean rolls into the basket and top with the pork tenderloins.
9. Air fry for another 7 minutes.
10. Remove from air fryer and transfer the pork tenderloins onto a platter.
11. Cut each tenderloin into desired size slices.
12. Serve alongside the potatoes and green beans rolls.

Nutrition:
- Calories: 918
- Carbohydrate: 42.4 g
- Protein: 77.9 g
- Fat: 47.7 g
- Sugar: 4 g
- Sodium: 1,400 mg

78. Pork Rolls

Preparation time: 20 minutes
Cooking time: 15 minutes
Servings: 4
Ingredients:
- 1 scallion, chopped
- 1/4 cup sun-dried tomatoes, finely chopped
- 2 tbsps. fresh parsley, chopped
- Salt and ground black pepper, as required
- 4 6-oz. pork cutlets, pounded slightly
- 2 tsps. paprika
- 1/2 tbsp. olive oil

Directions:
1. In a bowl, mix well scallion, tomatoes, parsley, salt, and black pepper.
2. Spread the tomato mixture over each pork cutlet.
3. Roll each cutlet and secure it with cocktail sticks.
4. Rub the outer part of the rolls with paprika, salt, and black pepper.
5. Coat the rolls evenly with oil.
6. Set the temperature of the air fryer to 390°F. Grease an air fryer basket.
7. Arrange pork rolls into the prepared air fryer basket in a single layer.
8. Air fry for about 15 minutes.
9. Remove from air fryer and transfer the pork rolls onto serving plates.
10. Serve hot.

Nutrition:
- Calories: 244
- Carbohydrate: 14.5 g
- Protein: 20.1 g
- Fat: 8.2 g
- Sugar: 1.7 g

79. Pork Sausage Casserole

Preparation time: 15 minutes
Cooking time: 30 minutes
Servings: 4
Ingredients:
- 6 oz. flour, sifted
- 2 eggs
- 1 red onion, thinly sliced
- 1 garlic clove, minced
- Salt and ground black pepper, as required
- 3/4 cup milk
- 2/3 cup cold water
- 8 small sausages
- 8 fresh rosemary sprigs

Directions:
1. In a bowl, mix together the flour and eggs.
2. Add the onion, garlic, salt, and black pepper. Mix them well.
3. Gently, add in the milk and water and mix until well combined.
4. In each sausage, pierce 1 rosemary sprig.
5. Set the temperature of the air fryer to 320°F. Grease a baking dish.
6. Arrange sausages into the prepared baking dish and top evenly with the flour mixture.
7. Air fry for about 30 minutes.
8. Remove from the air fryer and serve warm.

Nutrition:
- Calories: 334
- Carbohydrate: 37.7 g
- Protein: 14 g
- Fat: 14 g
- Sugar: 3.5 g
- Sodium: 250 mg

80. Lemon Chili Salmon

Preparation time: 10 minutes
Cooking time: 17 minutes
Servings: 2
Ingredients:
- 2 lbs. salmon fillet, skinless and boneless
- 2 lemon juice
- 1 orange juice
- 1 tablespoon olive oil
- 1 bunch fresh dill
- 1 chili, sliced
- Pepper
- Salt

Directions:
1. Preheat the air fryer to 325° F.
2. Place salmon fillets in an air fryer baking pan and drizzle with olive oil, lemon juice, and orange juice.
3. Sprinkle chili slices over salmon and season with pepper and salt.
4. Place pan in the air fryer and cook for 15-17 minutes.
5. Garnish with dill and serve.

Nutrition:
- Calories: 339
- Fat: 17.5 g
- Carbohydrates: 2 g
- Sugar 2 g
- Protein: 44 g

81. Tuna Burgers

Preparation time: 5 minutes
Cooking time: 6 minutes
Servings: 4
Ingredients:
- 7 Oz canned tuna
- 1 large egg
- 1/4 cup breadcrumbs
- 1 tbsp. Mustard
- 1/4 tsp garlic powder
- 1/4 tsp onion powder
- 1/4 tsp cayenne pepper
- Salt and ground black pepper, as required

Directions:
1. Add all the ingredients into a bowl and mix until well combined. Make 4 equal-sized patties from the mixture.
2. Arrange the patties onto a greased cooking rack. Arrange the drip pan in the bottom of the Air Fryer Oven cooking chamber. Select "Air Fry" and then adjust the temperature to 400 °F. Set the time for 6 minutes and press "Start."
3. When the display shows "Add Food" insert the cooking rack in the center position.
4. When the display shows "Turn Food" turn the burgers.
5. When the cooking time is complete, remove the tray from the Air fryer oven. Serve hot.

Nutrition:
- Calories: 151
- Carbohydrates: 6.3 g
- Fat: 6.4 g
- Protein: 16.4 g

82. Breaded Cod

Preparation time: 5 minutes
Cooking time: 10 minutes
Servings: 4
Ingredients:
- 1/3 cup all-purpose flour
- Ground black pepper, as required
- 1 large egg
- 2 tbsp water
- 2/3 cup cornflakes, crushed
- 1 tbsp parmesan cheese, grated
- 1/8 tsp cayenne pepper
- 1 lb. Cod fillets
- Salt, as required

Directions:
1. In a shallow dish, add the flour and black pepper and mix well. In a second shallow dish, add the egg and water and beat well. In a third shallow dish, add the cornflakes, cheese, and cayenne pepper and mix well.
2. Season the cod fillets with salt evenly. Coat the fillets with flour mixture, then dip into the egg mixture and finally coat with the cornflake mixture.
3. Arrange the cod fillets onto the greased cooking rack. Arrange the drip pan in the bottom of the Air Fryer Oven cooking chamber. Select "Air Fry" and then adjust the temperature to 400 °F. Set the time for 10 minutes and press "Start."
4. When the display shows "Add Food" insert the cooking rack in the bottom position. When the display shows "Turn Food" turn the cod fillets. When cooking time is complete, remove the tray from the Air fryer oven. Serve hot.

Nutrition:
- Calories: 168
- Carbohydrates: 12.1 g
- Fat: 2.7 g
- Protein: 23.7 g

83. Salmon Patties

Preparation time: 10 minutes
Cooking time: 7 minutes
Servings: 2
Ingredients:
- 8 oz. salmon fillet, minced
- 1 lemon, sliced
- 1/2 teaspoon garlic powder
- 1 egg lightly beaten
- 1/8 teaspoon salt

Directions:
1. Add all ingredients except lemon slices into the bowl and mix until well combined.
2. Spray air fryer basket with cooking spray.
3. Place lemon slice into the air fryer basket.
4. Make the equal shape of patties from the salmon mixture and place on top of lemon slices into the air fryer basket.
5. Cook at 390 F for 7 minutes.

6. Serve and enjoy.

Nutrition:
- Calories: 184
- Fat: 9.2 g
- Carbohydrates: 1 g
- Sugar 0.4 g
- Protein: 24.9 g

84. Spicy Catfish

Preparation time: 5 minutes
Cooking time: 15 minutes
Servings: 4
Ingredients:
- 2 tbsp cornmeal polenta
- 2 tsp cajun seasoning
- 1/2 tsp paprika
- 1/2 tsp garlic powder
- Salt, as required
- 2 (6-oz) catfish fillets
- 1 tbsp olive oil

Directions:
1. In a bowl, mix the cornmeal, Cajun seasoning paprika, garlic powder, and salt. Add the catfish fillets and coat evenly with the mixture. Now, coat each fillet with oil.
2. Arrange the fish fillets onto a greased cooking rack and spray with cooking spray. Arrange the drip pan in the bottom of the Air Fryer Oven cooking chamber. Select "Air Fry" and then adjust the temperature to 400 °F. Set the timer for 14 minutes and press "Start."
3. When the display shows "Add Food" insert the cooking rack in the center position. When the display shows "Turn Food" turn the fillets.
4. When cooking time is complete, remove the rack from the Air fryer oven. Serve hot.

Nutrition:
- Calories: 32 Carbohydrates: 6.7 g
- Fat: 20.3 g
- Protein: 27.3 g

85. Vinegar Halibut

Preparation time: 5 minutes
Cooking time: 12 minutes
Servings: 2
Ingredients:
- 2 (5-oz) halibut fillets
- 1 garlic clove, minced
- 1 tsp fresh rosemary, minced
- 1 tbsp olive oil
- 1 tbsp red wine vinegar
- 1/8 tsp hot sauce

Directions:
1. In a large resealable bag add all ingredients. Seal the bag and shale well to mix. Refrigerate to marinate for at least 30 minutes. Remove the fish fillets from the bag and shake off the excess marinade. Arrange the halibut fillets onto the greased cooking tray.
2. Arrange the drip pan in the bottom of the Air Fryer Oven cooking chamber. Select "Bake" and then adjust the temperature to 450 °F. Set the time for 12 minutes and press "Start." When the display shows "Add Food" insert the cooking tray in the center position. When the display shows "Turn Food" turn the halibut fillets. When the cooking time is complete, remove the tray from the Air fryer oven. Serve hot.

Nutrition:
- Calories: 223
- Carbohydrates: 1 g
- Fat: 10.4 g
- Protein: 30 g

86. Lemony Salmon

Preparation time: 5 minutes
Cooking time: 10 minutes
Servings: 2
Ingredients:
- 1 tbsp. of fresh lemon juice
- 1/2 tbsp olive oil
- Salt and ground black pepper, as required
- 1 garlic clove, minced
- 1/2 tsp. fresh thyme leaves, chopped
- 2 (7-oz) salmon fillets

Directions:
1. In a bowl, add all ingredients except the salmon and mix well. Add the salmon fillets and coat with the mixture generously.
2. Arrange the salmon fillets onto a lightly greased cooking rack, skin-side down. Arrange the drip pan in the bottom of the Air Fryer Oven cooking chamber. Select "Air Fry" and then adjust the temperature to 400

°F. Set the time for 10 minutes and press "Start."
3. When the display shows "Add Food" insert the cooking rack in the bottom position. When the display shows "Turn Food" turn the fillets.
4. When the cooking time is complete, remove the tray from the Air fryer oven. Serve hot.

Nutrition:
- Calories: 297
- Carbohydrates: 0.8 g
- Fat: 15.8 g
- Protein: 38.7 g

87. Spiced Tilapia

Preparation time: 5 minutes
Cooking time: 12 minutes
Servings: 2
Ingredients:
- 1/2 Tsp lemon pepper seasoning
- 1/2 tsp. Garlic powder
- 1/2 tsp onion powder
- Salt and ground black pepper, as required
- 2 (6-oz) tilapia fillets
- 1 tbsp olive oil

Directions:
1. In a small bowl, mix the spices, salt, and black pepper. Coat the tilapia fillets with oil and then rub with spice mixture. Arrange the tilapia fillets onto a lightly greased cooking rack, skin-side down.
2. Arrange the drip pan in the bottom of the Air Fryer Oven cooking chamber. Select "Air Fry" and then adjust the temperature to 360 °F. Set the time for 12 minutes and press "Start."
3. When the display shows "Add Food" insert the cooking rack in the bottom position. When the display shows "Turn Food" turn the fillets.
4. When the cooking time is complete, remove the tray from the Air fryer oven. Serve hot.

Nutrition:
- Calories: 206
- Carbohydrates: 0.2 g
- Fat: 8.6 g
- Protein: 31.9 g

88. Buttered Salmon

Preparation time: 5 minutes
Cooking time: 10 minutes
Servings: 2
Ingredients:
- 2 salmon fillets (6-oz)
- Salt and ground black pepper, as required
- 1 tbsp butter, melted

Directions:
1. Season each salmon fillet with salt and black pepper and then, coat with the butter. Arrange the salmon fillets onto the greased cooking tray.
2. Arrange the drip pan in the bottom of the Air Fryer Oven cooking chamber. Select "Air Fry" and then adjust the temperature to 360 °F. Set the time for 10 minutes and press "Start."
3. When the display shows "Add Food" insert the cooking tray in the center position. When the display shows "Turn Food" turn the salmon fillets.
4. When cooking time is complete, remove the tray from the Air fryer oven. Serve hot.

Nutrition:
- Calories: 276
- Carbohydrates: 0 g
- Fat: 16.3 g
- Protein: 33.1 g

89. Crispy Fish Sticks in Air Fryer

Preparation time: 10 minutes
Cooking time: 15 minutes
Servings: 2
Ingredients:
- Whitefish such as cod 1 lb.
- Mayonnaise 1/4 c
- Dijon mustard 2 tbsp.
- Water 2 tbsp.
- Pork rind 1&1/2 c
- Cajun seasoning 3/4 tsp
- Kosher salt & pepper to taste

Directions:
1. Spray non-stick cooking spray to the air fryer rack.
2. Pat the fish dry & cut into sticks about 1 inch by 2 inches' broad

3. Stir together the mayo, mustard, and water in a tiny small dish. Mix the pork rinds & Cajun seasoning into another small container.
4. Adding kosher salt & pepper to taste (both pork rinds & seasoning can have a decent amount of kosher salt, so you can dip a finger to see how salty it is).
5. Working for one slice of fish at a time, dip to cover in the mayo mix & then tap off the excess. Dip into the mixture of pork rind, then flip to cover. Place on the rack of an air fryer.
6. Set at 400° F to Air Fry & bake for 5 minutes, then turn the fish with tongs and bake for another 5 minutes. Serve.

Nutrition:
- Calories: 263 Fat: 16 g
- Net Carbohydrates: 1 g
- Protein: 26.4 g

90. Honey-Glazed Salmon

Preparation time: 10 minutes
Cooking time: 15 minutes
Servings: 2
Ingredients:
- 6 tsp Gluten-free Soy Sauce
- 2 pcs Salmon Fillets
- 3 tsp Sweet rice wine
- 1 tsp Water
- 6 tbsp Honey

Directions:
1. In a bowl, mix sweet rice wine, soy sauce, honey, and water.
2. Set half of it aside.
3. In the half of it, marinate the fish and let it rest for two hours.
4. Let the air fryer preheat to 180° C
5. Cook the fish for 8 minutes, flip halfway through and cook for another five minutes.
6. Baste the salmon with marinade mixture after 3 or 4 minutes.
7. The half of marinade, pour in a saucepan reduce to half, serve with a sauce.

Nutrition:
- Calories 254
- Carbs 9.9 g
- Fat 12 g
- Protein 20 g

91. Basil-Parmesan Crusted Salmon

Preparation time: 5 minutes
Cooking time: 15 minutes
Servings: 4
Ingredients:
- Grated Parmesan: 3 tablespoons
- Skinless four salmon fillets
- Salt: 1/4 teaspoon
- Freshly ground black pepper
- Low-fat mayonnaise: 3 tablespoons
- Basil leaves, chopped
- Half lemon

Directions:
1. Let the air fryer preheat to 400° F. Spray the basket with olive oil.
2. With salt, pepper, and lemon juice, season the salmon.
3. In a bowl, mix two tablespoons of Parmesan cheese with mayonnaise and basil leaves.
4. Add this mix and more parmesan on top of salmon and cook for seven minutes or until fully cooked.
5. Serve hot.

Nutrition:
- Calories: 289
- Carbohydrates: 1.5 g
- Protein: 30 g
- Fat: 18.5 g

92. Halibut Ceviche with Cilantro

Preparation time: 10 minutes
Cooking time: 0 minutes
Servings: 4
Ingredients:
- 1/2 pound (227 g) fresh skinless, white, ocean fish fillet (halibut, mahi mahi, etc.), diced
- 1 cup freshly squeezed lime juice, divided
- 2 tablespoons chopped fresh cilantro, divided
- 1 Serrano pepper, sliced
- 1 garlic clove, crushed
- 3/4 teaspoon salt, divided
- 1/2 red onion, thinly sliced
- 2 tomatoes, diced
- 1 red bell pepper, seeded and diced
- 1 tablespoon extra-virgin olive oil

Directions:
1. In a large mixing bowl, combine the fish, 3/4 cup of lime juice, 1 tablespoon of cilantro, Serrano pepper, garlic, and 1/2 teaspoon of salt.
2. The fish should be covered or nearly covered in lime juice. Cover the bowl and refrigerate for 4 hours.
3. Sprinkle the remaining 1/4 teaspoon of salt over the onion in a small bowl, and let sit for 10 minutes. Drain and rinse well.
4. In a large bowl, combine the tomatoes, bell pepper, olive oil, remaining 1/4 cup of lime juice, and onion. Let rest for at least 10 minutes, or as long as 4 hours, while the fish "cooks."
5. When the fish is ready, it will be completely white and opaque. At this time, strain the juice, reserving it in another bowl. If desired, remove the Serrano pepper and garlic.
6. Add the vegetables to the fish, and stir gently. Taste, and add some of the reserved lime juice to the ceviche as desired.
7. Serve topped with the remaining 1 tablespoon of cilantro.

Nutrition:
- Calories: 122
- Fat: 4.1 g
- Protein: 11.9 g
- Carbs: 11.1 g
- Fiber: 2.1 g
- Sugar: 4.9 g
- Sodium: 404 mg

93. Ginger Cod Chard Bake

Preparation time: 10 minutes
Cooking time: 15 minutes
Servings: 4
Ingredients:
- 1 chard bunch, stemmed, leaves and stems cut into thin strips
- 1 red bell pepper, seeded and cut into strips
- 1 pound (454 g) cod fillets cut into 4 pieces
- 1 tablespoon grated fresh ginger
- 3 garlic cloves, minced
- 2 tablespoons white wine vinegar
- 2 tablespoons low-sodium tamari or gluten-free soy sauce
- 1/2 tablespoon honey

Directions:
1. Preheat the oven to 425°F (220°C).
2. Cut four pieces of parchment paper, each about 16 inches wide. Lay the four pieces out on a large workspace.
3. On each piece of paper, arrange a small pile of chard leaves and stems, topped by several strips of bell pepper. Top with a piece of cod.
4. In a small bowl, mix the ginger, garlic, vinegar, tamari, and honey. Top each piece of fish with one-fourth of the mixture.
5. Fold the parchment paper over so the edges overlap. Fold the edges over several times to secure the fish in the packets. Carefully place the packets on a large baking sheet.
6. Bake for 12 minutes. Carefully open the packets, allowing steam to escape, and serve.

Nutrition:
- Calories: 120
- Fat: 1.0 g
- Protein: 19.1 g
- Carbs: 8.9 g
- Fiber: 1.1 g
- Sugar: 6.1 g
- Sodium: 716 mg

94. Peppery Halibut Fillet with Beans

Preparation time: 10 minutes
Cooking time: 15 minutes
Servings: 4
Ingredients:
- 1 pound (454 g) green beans, trimmed
- 2 red bell peppers, seeded and cut into strips
- 1 onion, sliced
- Zest and juice of 2 lemons
- 3 garlic cloves, minced
- 2 tablespoons extra-virgin olive oil
- 1 teaspoon dried dill
- 1 teaspoon dried oregano
- 4 (4-ounce / 113-g) halibut fillets
- 1/2 teaspoon salt
- 1/4 teaspoons freshly ground black pepper

Directions:
1. Preheat the oven to 400°F (205°C). Line a baking sheet with parchment paper.
2. In a large bowl, toss the green beans, bell peppers, onion, lemon zest and juice, garlic, olive oil, dill, and oregano.
3. Use a slotted spoon to transfer the vegetables to the prepared baking sheet in a single layer, leaving the juice behind in the bowl.
4. Gently place the halibut fillets in the bowl, and coat in the juice.
5. Transfer the fillets to the baking sheet, nestled between the vegetables, and drizzle them with any juice left in the bowl.
6. Sprinkle the vegetables and halibut with the salt and pepper.
7. Bake for 15 to 20 minutes until the vegetables are just tender and the fish flakes apart easily.

Nutrition:
- Calories: 235
- Fat: 9.1 g
- Protein: 23.9 g
- Carbs: 16.1 g
- Fiber: 4.9 g
- Sugar: 8.1 g
- Sodium: 350 mg

95. Fruity Cod with Salsa

Preparation time: 10 minutes
Cooking time: 10 minutes
Servings: 4
Ingredients:
- 1 pound (454 g) cod, cut into 4 fillets, pin bones removed
- 2 tablespoons extra-virgin olive oil
- 3/4 teaspoon sea salt, divided
- 1 mango, pitted, peeled, and cut into cubes
- 1/4 cup chopped cilantro
- 1/2 red onion, finely chopped
- 1 jalapeño, seeded and finely chopped
- 1 garlic clove, minced
- Juice of 1 lime

Directions:
1. Preheat the oven broiler on high.
2. On a rimmed baking sheet, brush the cod with the olive oil and season with 1/2 teaspoon of the salt. Broil until the fish is opaque, 5 to 10 minutes.
3. Meanwhile, in a small bowl, combine the mango, cilantro, onion, jalapeño, garlic, lime juice, and remaining 1/4 teaspoon of salt.
4. Serve the cod with the salsa spooned over the top.

Nutrition:
- Calories: 200 Fat: 8.0 g
- Protein: 21.1 g Carbs: 12.9 g
- Fiber: 1.9 g Sugar: 7.6 g Sodium: 355 mg

96. Broiled Cod Fillets with Garlic Mango Salsa

Preparation time: 10 minutes
Cooking time: 5 to 10 minutes
Servings: 4
Ingredients:
Cod:
- 1 pound (454 g) cod, cut into 4 fillets, pin bones removed
- 2 tablespoons extra-virgin olive oil
- 3/4 teaspoon sea salt, divided

Mango Salsa:
- 1 mango, pitted, peeled, and cut into cubes
- 1/4 cup chopped cilantro
- 1 jalapeño, deseeded and finely chopped
- 1/2 red onion, finely chopped
- Juice of 1 lime
- 1 garlic clove, minced

Directions:
1. Preheat the broiler to high. Place the cod fillets on a rimmed baking sheet. Brush both sides of the fillets with the olive oil. Sprinkle with 1/2 teaspoon of the salt.
2. Broil in the preheated broiler for 5 to 10 minutes until the flesh flakes easily with a fork.
3. Meanwhile, make the mango salsa by stirring together the mango, cilantro, jalapeño, red onion, lime juice, garlic, and remaining salt in a small bowl.
4. Serve the cod warm topped with the mango salsa.

Nutrition:
- Calories: 198 Fat: 8.1 g
- Protein: 21.2 g Carbs: 13.2 g
- Fiber: 2.2 g Saturated fat: 1 g
- Sodium: 355 mg

97. Butter Cod with Lemony Asparagus

Preparation time: 5 minutes
Cooking time: 10 minutes
Servings: 4
Ingredients:
- 4 (4-ounce / 113-g) cod fillets
- 1/4 teaspoon garlic powder
- 1/4 teaspoon salt
- 1/4 teaspoons freshly ground black pepper
- 2 tablespoons unsalted butter
- 24 asparagus spears, woody ends trimmed
- 1/2 cup brown rice, cooked
- 1 tablespoon freshly squeezed lemon juice

Directions:
1. In a large bowl, season the cod fillets with the garlic powder, salt, and pepper. Set aside.
2. Melt the butter in a skillet over medium-low heat.
3. Place the cod fillets and asparagus in the skillet in a single layer. Cook covered for 8 minutes, or until the cod is cooked through.
4. Divide the cooked brown rice, cod fillets, and asparagus among four plates. Serve drizzled with the lemon juice.

Nutrition:
- Calories: 233 Fat: 8.2 g
- Protein: 22.1 g
- Carbs: 20.1 g
- Fiber: 5.2 g
- Sugar: 2.2 g
- Sodium: 275 mg

98. Cod Fillet Quinoa Asparagus Bowl

Preparation time: 5 minutes
Cooking time: 15 minutes
Servings: 4
Ingredients:
- 1/2 cup uncooked quinoa
- 4 (4-ounce / 113-g) cod fillets
- 1/2 teaspoon garlic powder, divided
- 1/4 teaspoon salt
- 1/4 teaspoons freshly ground black pepper
- 24 asparagus spears cut the bottom 1 1/2 inches off
- 1 tablespoon avocado oil
- 1 cup half-and-half

Directions:
1. Put the quinoa in a pot of salted water. Bring to a boil. Reduce the heat to low and simmer for 15 minutes or until the quinoa is soft and has a white "tail." Cover and turn off the heat. Let sit for 5 minutes.
2. On a clean work surface, rub the cod fillets with 1/4 teaspoon of garlic powder, salt, and pepper.
3. Heat the avocado oil in a non-stick skillet over medium-low heat.
4. Add the cod fillets and asparagus in the skillet and cook for 8 minutes or until they are tender. Flip the cod and shake the skillet halfway through the cooking time.
5. Pour the half-and-half in the skillet, and sprinkle with remaining garlic powder. Turn up the heat to high and simmer for 2 minutes until creamy.
6. Divide the quinoa, cod fillets, and asparagus in four bowls and serve warm.

Nutrition:
- Calories: 258
- Fat: 7.9 g
- Protein: 25.2 g
- Carbs: 22.7 g
- Fiber: 5.2 g
- Sugar: 3.8 g
- Sodium: 410 mg

99. Tuna Onion Broccoli Casserole

Preparation time: 10 minutes
Cooking time: 40 minutes
Servings: 4
Ingredients:
- 1 tablespoon avocado oil
- 1 medium yellow onion, diced
- 2 tablespoons whole-wheat flour
- 2 cups low-sodium chicken broth
- 1 cup unsweetened almond milk
- 1 (10-ounce / 284-g) package zucchini noodles
- 1 cup fresh or frozen broccoli, cut into florets
- 2 (5-ounce / 142-g) cans chunk-light tuna, drained
- 1 cup Cheddar cheese, shredded

Directions:
1. Preheat the oven to 375°F (190°C). Heat the avocado oil in a nonstick skillet over medium heat until shimmering.
2. Add the onion to the skillet and cook for 3 minutes or until translucent.
3. Add the flour to the skillet and cook for 2 minutes. Stir constantly.
4. Gently fold in the chicken broth and almond milk, then turn up the heat to high and bring the mixture to a boil.
5. Add the zucchini noodles and broccoli to the skillet. Reduce the heat to medium and cook for 6 minutes until the mixture is lightly thickened. Add the tuna to the skillet.
6. Pour the mixture in a casserole dish, and spread the cheese on top. Cover the casserole dish with aluminum foil.
7. Bake in the preheated oven for 20 minutes or until the tuna is opaque. Remove the aluminum foil and broil for an additional 2 minutes.
8. Remove the casserole from the oven. Allow to cool for a few minutes and serve warm.

Nutrition:
- Calories: 273
- Fat: 11.8 g
- Protein: 29.1 g
- Carbs: 11.1 g
- Fiber: 3.2 g
- Sugar: 2.8 g
- Sodium: 349 mg

CHAPTER 8:

Side Dish Recipes

100. Coffee-Steamed Carrots

Preparation time: 10 minutes
Cooking time: 3 minutes
Servings: 4
Ingredients:
- 1 cup brewed coffee
- 1 tsp. light brown sugar
- 1/2 tsp. Kosher salt
- Freshly ground black pepper
- 1 lb. baby carrots
- Fresh parsley, chopped
- 1 tsp. grated lemon zest

Directions:
1. Pour the coffee into the electric pressure cooker. Stir in the brown sugar, salt, and pepper. Add the carrots.
2. Close the pressure cooker. Set to sealing.
3. Cook on high pressure for minutes.
4. Once complete, click Cancel and quickly release the pressure.
5. Once the pin drops, open and remove the lid.
6. Using a slotted spoon, portion carrots to a serving bowl. Topped with the parsley and lemon zest, and serve.

Nutrition:
- Calories: 51
- Carbohydrates: 12 g
- Fiber: 4 g

101. Rosemary Potatoes

Preparation time: 5 minutes
Cooking time: 25 minutes
Servings: 2
Ingredients:
- 1 lb. red potatoes
- 1 cup vegetable stock
- 2 tbsp. olive oil
- 2 tbsp. Rosemary sprigs

Directions:
1. Situate potatoes in the steamer basket and add the stock into the Instant Pot.
2. Steam the potatoes in your Instant Pot for 15 minutes.
3. Depressurize and pour away the remaining stock.
4. Set to sauté and add the oil, rosemary, and potatoes.
5. Cook until brown.

Nutrition:
- Calories: 195 Carbohydrates: 31 g
- Fat: 1 g

102. Wonderful Steamed Artichoke

Preparation time: 5 minutes
Cooking time: 4 hours
Servings: 4
Ingredients:
- 8 medium-sized artichokes, stemmed and trimmed
- 2 tsp. salt
- 4 tbsp. lemon juice

Directions:
1. Cut 1-inch part of the artichoke from the top and place it in a 6-quarts slow cooker, facing an upright position. Using a bowl, place the lemon juice and pour in the salt until it mixes properly.
2. Pour this mixture over the artichoke and add the water to cover at least 3/4 of the artichokes.
3. Cover the top, switch on the slow cooker; place the cooking time to 4 hours, then cook at a high heat setting. Serve immediately.

Nutrition:
- Calories: 78 Carbohydrates: 17 g
- Protein: 5 g

103. Mashed Pumpkin

Preparation time: 9 minutes
Cooking time: 15 minutes
Servings: 2
Ingredients:
- 2 cups chopped pumpkin
- 1/2 cup water
- 2 tbsp. powdered sugar-free sweetener of choice
- 1 tbsp. cinnamon

Directions:
1. Place the pumpkin and water in your Instant Pot. Seal and cook on Stew for 15 minutes.
2. Remove and mash with the sweetener and cinnamon.

Nutrition:
- Calories: 12 Carbohydrates: 3 g
- Sugar: 1 g

104. Parmesan-Topped Acorn Squash

Preparation time: 8 minutes
Cooking time: 20 minutes
Servings: 4
Ingredients:

- 1 acorn squash (about 1 pound)
- 1 tbsp. extra-virgin olive oil
- 1 tsp. dried sage leaves, crumbled
- 1/4 tsp. freshly grated nutmeg
- 1/8 tsp. Kosher salt
- 1/8 tsp. freshly ground black pepper
- 2 tbsp. freshly grated Parmesan cheese

Directions:

1. Chop acorn squash in half lengthwise and remove the seeds. Cut each half in half for a total of 4 wedges. Snap off the stem if it's easy to do.
2. In a small bowl, combine the olive oil, sage, nutmeg salt, and pepper. Brush the cut sides of the squash with the olive oil mixture.
3. Fill 1 cup water into the electric pressure cooker and insert a wire rack or trivet.
4. Place the squash on the trivet in a single layer, skin-side down.
5. Set the lid of the pressure cooker on sealing.
6. Cook on high pressure for 20 minutes.
7. Once done, press cancel and quickly release the pressure.
8. Once the pin drops, open it.
9. Carefully remove the squash from the pot, sprinkle with the Parmesan, and serve.

Nutrition:

- Calories: 85
- Carbohydrates: 12 g
- Fiber: 2 g

105. Low Fat Roasties

Preparation time: 8 minutes
Cooking time: 25 minutes
Servings: 2
Ingredients:

- 1 lb. roasting potatoes
- 1 garlic clove
- 1 cup vegetable stock
- 2 tbsp. olive oil

Directions:

1. Position potatoes in the steamer basket and add the stock into the Instant Pot.
2. Steam the potatoes in your Instant Pot for 15 minutes.
3. Depressurize and pour away the remaining stock.
4. Set to sauté and add the oil, garlic, and potatoes. Cook until brown.

Nutrition:

- Calories: 201
- Carbohydrates: 3 g
- Fat: 6 g

106. Roasted Parsnips

Preparation time: 9 minutes
Cooking time: 25 minutes
Servings: 2
Ingredients:

- 1 lb. parsnips
- 1 cup vegetable stock
- 2 tbsp. herbs
- 2 tbsp. olive oil

Directions:

1. Put the parsnips in the steamer basket and add the stock into the Instant Pot.
2. Steam the parsnips in your Instant Pot for 15 minutes.
3. Depressurize and pour away the remaining stock.
4. Set to sauté and add the oil, herbs, and parsnips.
5. Cook until golden and crisp.

Nutrition:

- Calories: 130
- Carbohydrates: 14 g
- Protein: 4 g

107. Lower Carb Hummus

Preparation time: 9 minutes
Cooking time: 60 minutes
Servings: 2
Ingredients:

- 1/2 cup dry chickpeas
- 1 cup vegetable stock
- 1 cup pumpkin puree
- 2 tbsp. smoked paprika
- Salt and pepper to taste

Directions:
1. Soak the chickpeas overnight.
2. Place the chickpeas and stock in the Instant Pot.
3. Cook on Beans for 60 minutes.
4. Depressurize naturally.
5. Blend the chickpeas with the remaining ingredients.

Nutrition:
- Calories: 135
- Carbohydrates: 18 g
- Fat: 3 g

108. Parmesan Cauliflower Mash

Preparation time: 19 minutes
Cooking time: 5 minutes
Servings: 4
Ingredients:
- 1 head cauliflower
- 1/2 tsp. Kosher salt
- 1/2 tsp. garlic pepper
- 2 tbsp. plain Greek yogurt
- 3/4 cup freshly grated Parmesan cheese
- 1 tbsp. unsalted butter or ghee (optional)
- Chopped fresh chives

Directions:
1. Pour cup water into the electric pressure cooker and insert a steamer basket or wire rack.
2. Place the cauliflower in the basket.
3. Cover lid of the pressure cooker to seal.
4. Cook on high pressure for 5 minutes.
5. Once complete, hit Cancel and quickly release the pressure.
6. When the pin drops, remove the lid.
7. Remove the cauliflower from the pot and pour out the water. Return the cauliflower to the pot and add the salt, garlic pepper, yogurt, and cheese. Use an immersion blender to purée or mash the cauliflower in the pot.
8. Spoon into a serving bowl, and garnish with butter (if using) and chives.

Nutrition:
- Calories: 141
- Carbohydrates: 12 g
- Fiber: 4 g

109. Steamed Asparagus

Preparation time: 3 minutes
Cooking time: 2 minutes
Servings: 4
Ingredients:
- 1 lb. fresh asparagus, rinsed and tough ends trimmed
- 1 cup water

Directions:
1. Place the asparagus into a wire steamer rack, and set it inside your Instant Pot.
2. Add water to the pot. Close and seal the lid, turning the steam release valve to the "Sealing" position.
3. Select the "Steam" function to cook on high pressure for 2 minutes.
4. Once done, do a quick pressure release of the steam.
5. Lift the wire steamer basket out of the pot and place the asparagus onto a serving plate.
6. Season as desired and serve.

Nutrition:
- Calories: 22 Carbohydrates: 4 g
- Protein: 2 g

110. Squash Medley

Preparation time: 10 minutes
Cooking time: 20 minutes.
Servings: 2
Ingredients:
- 2 lbs. mixed squash
- 1/2 cup mixed veg
- 1 cup vegetable stock
- 2 tbsp. olive oil
- 2 tbsp. mixed herbs

Directions:
1. Put the squash in the steamer basket and add the stock into the Instant Pot.
2. Steam the squash in your Instant Pot for 10 minutes.
3. Depressurize and pour away the remaining stock.
4. Set to sauté and add the oil and remaining ingredients.
5. Cook until a light crust forms.

Nutrition:
- Calories: 100 Carbohydrates: 10 g
- Fat: 6 g

111. Eggplant Curry

Preparation time: 15 minutes
Cooking time: 20 minutes
Servings: 2
Ingredients:

- 3 cups chopped eggplant
- 1 thinly sliced onion
- 1 cup coconut milk
- 3 tbsp. curry paste
- 1 tbsp. oil or ghee

Directions:

1. Select Instant Pot to sauté and put the onion, oil, and curry paste.
2. Once the onion is soft, stir in the remaining ingredients and seal.
3. Cook on Stew for 20 minutes. Release the pressure naturally.

Nutrition:

- Calories: 350
- Carbohydrates: 15 g
- Fat: 25 g

112. Lentil and Eggplant Stew

Preparation time: 15 minutes
Cooking time: 35 minutes
Servings: 2
Ingredients:

- 1 lb. eggplant
- 1 lb. dry lentils
- 1 cup chopped vegetables
- 1 cup low sodium vegetable broth

Directions:

1. Incorporate all the ingredients in your Instant Pot. Cook on Stew for 35 minutes.
2. Release the pressure naturally and serve.

Nutrition:

- Calories: 310
- Carbohydrates: 22 g
- Fat: 10 g

113. Tofu Curry

Preparation time: 15 minutes
Cooking time: 20 minutes
Servings: 2
Ingredients:

- 2 cups cubed extra firm tofu
- 2 cups mixed stir fry vegetables
- 1/2 cup soy yogurt
- 3 tbsp. curry paste
- 1 tbsp. oil or ghee

Directions:

1. Set the Instant Pot to sauté and add the oil and curry paste.
2. Once soft, place the remaining ingredients except for the yogurt and seal.
3. Cook on Stew for 20 minutes.
4. Release the pressure naturally and serve with a scoop of soy yogurt.

Nutrition:

- Calories: 300 Carbohydrates: 9 g
- Fat: 14 g

114. Lentil and Chickpea Curry

Preparation time: 15 minutes
Cooking time: 20 minutes
Servings: 2
Ingredients:

- 2 cups dry lentils and chickpeas
- 1 thinly sliced onion
- 1 cup chopped tomato
- 3 tbsp. curry paste
- 1 tbsp. oil or ghee

Directions:

1. Press Instant Pot to sauté and mix onion, oil, and curry paste.
2. Once the onion is cooked, stir the remaining ingredients and seal.
3. Cook on Stew for 20 minutes.
4. Release the pressure naturally and serve.

Nutrition:

- Calories: 360
- Carbohydrates: 26 g
- Fat: 19 g

115. Kidney Bean Stew

Preparation time: 15 minutes
Cooking time: 15 minutes
Servings: 2
Ingredients:

- 1 lb. cooked kidney beans
- 1 cup tomato passata
- 1 cup low sodium beef broth
- 3 tbsp. Italian herbs

Directions:
1. Incorporate all the ingredients in your Instant Pot, cook on Stew for 15 minutes.
2. Release the pressure naturally and serve.

Nutrition:
- Calories: 270 Carbohydrates: 16 g
- Fat: 10 g

116. Fried Tofu Hotpot

Preparation time: 15 minutes
Cooking time: 15 minutes
Servings: 2
Ingredients:
- 1/2 lb. fried tofu
- 1 lb. chopped Chinese vegetable mix
- 1 cup low sodium vegetable broth
- 2 tbsp. 5 spice seasoning
- 1 tbsp. smoked paprika

Directions:
1. Combine all the ingredients in your Instant Pot, set on Stew for 15 minutes.
2. Release the pressure naturally and serve.

Nutrition:
- Calories: 320 Carbohydrates: 11 g
- Fat: 23 g

117. Chili Sin Carne

Preparation time: 15 minutes
Cooking time: 35 minutes
Servings: 2
Ingredients:
- 3 cups mixed cooked beans
- 2 cups chopped tomatoes
- 1 tbsp. yeast extract
- 2 squares very dark chocolate
- 1 tbsp. red chili flakes

Directions:
1. Combine all the ingredients in your Instant Pot, cook for 35 minutes.
2. Release the pressure naturally and serve.

Nutrition:
- Calories: 240
- Carbohydrates: 20 g
- Fat: 3 g

118. Carrot Hummus

Preparation time: 15 minutes
Cooking time: 10 minutes
Servings: 2
Ingredients:
- 1 chopped carrot
- 2 oz. cooked chickpeas
- 1 tsp. lemon juice
- 1 tsp. tahini
- 1 tsp. fresh parsley

Directions:
1. Place the carrot and chickpeas in your Instant Pot.
2. Add a cup of water, seal, cook for 10 minutes on the Stew.
3. Depressurize naturally. Blend with the remaining ingredients.

Nutrition:
- Calories: 58
- Carbohydrates: 8 g
- Fat: 2 g

119. Garlic Sautéed Spinach

Preparation time: 5 minutes
Cooking time: 10 minutes
Servings: 4
Ingredients:
- 1 1/2 tbsp. olive oil
- 4 cloves minced garlic
- 6 cups fresh baby spinach
- Salt and pepper

Directions:
1. Heat up oil in a huge skillet over medium-high heat.
2. Add the garlic and cook for 1 minute.
3. Stir in the spinach and season with salt and pepper.
4. Sauté for 1 to 2 minutes until just wilted. Serve hot.

Nutrition:
- Calories: 60
- Carbohydrates: 2.6 g
- Fat: 1.1 g

CHAPTER 9:

Salad Recipes

120. Tomato, Cucumber, and Avocado Salad

Preparation time: 10 minutes
Cooking time: 0 minutes
Servings: 4
Ingredients:
- 1 cup cherry tomatoes, halved
- 1 large cucumber, chopped
- 1 small red onion, thinly sliced
- 1 avocado, diced
- 2 tablespoons chopped fresh dill
- 2 tablespoons extra-virgin olive oil
- Juice of 1 lemon
- 1/4 teaspoon salt
- 1/4 teaspoon freshly ground black pepper

Directions:
1. In a large mixing bowl, combine the tomatoes, cucumber, onion, avocado, and dill.
2. In a small bowl, combine the oil, lemon juice, salt, and pepper, and mix well.
3. Drizzle the dressing over the vegetables and toss to combine. Serve.

Nutrition:
- Calories: 152
- Fat: 12.1 g
- Protein: 2.1 g
- Carbohydrates: 10.9 g
- Fiber: 4.1 g
- Sugar: 4.0 g

121. Green Salad with Blackberries Vinaigrette

Preparation time: 15 minutes
Cooking time: 20 minutes
Servings: 4
Ingredients:
For the Vinaigrette:
- 1 pint blackberries
- 2 tablespoons red wine vinegar
- 1 tablespoon honey
- 3 tablespoons extra-virgin olive oil
- 1/4 teaspoon salt
- Freshly ground black pepper

For the Salad:
- 1 sweet potato, cubed
- 1 teaspoon extra-virgin olive oil
- 8 cups salad greens (baby spinach, spicy greens, romaine)
- 1/2 red onion, sliced
- 1/4 cup crumbled goat cheese

Directions:
To Make the Vinaigrette:
1. In a blender jar, combine the blackberries, vinegar, honey, oil, salt, and pepper, and process until smooth. Set aside.

To Make the Salad:
1. Preheat the oven to 425°F (220°C). Line a baking sheet with parchment paper.
2. In a medium mixing bowl, toss the sweet potato with the olive oil. Transfer to the prepared baking sheet and roast for 20 minutes, stirring once halfway through, until tender. Remove and cool for a few minutes.
3. In a large bowl, toss the greens with the red onion and cooled sweet potato, and drizzle with the vinaigrette. Serve topped with 1 tablespoon of goat cheese per serving.

Nutrition:
- Calories: 197 Fat: 12.1 g
- Protein: 3.1 g
- Carbohydrates: 20.9 g
- Fiber: 6.1 g
- Sugar: 10.0 g

122. Summer Salad with Honey Dressing

Preparation time: 5 minutes
Cooking time: 0 minutes
Servings: 4
Ingredients:
For the Salad:
- 8 cups mixed greens or preferred lettuce, loosely packed
- 4 cups arugula, loosely packed
- 2 peaches, sliced 1/2 cup thinly sliced red onion
- 1/2 cup chopped walnuts or pecans
- 1/2 cup crumbled feta

For the Dressing:
- 4 teaspoons extra-virgin olive oil
- 4 teaspoons honey

Directions:
To Make the Salad:
1. Combine the mixed greens, arugula, peaches, red onion, walnuts, and feta in a large bowl. Divide the salad into four portions.
2. Drizzle the dressing over each individual serving of salad.

To Make the Dressing:
1. In a small bowl, whisk together the olive oil and honey.

Nutrition:
- Calories: 264
- Fat: 18.1 g
- Protein: 8.1 g
- Carbohydrates: 21.9 g
- Fiber: 5.1 g
- Sugar: 16.0 g

123. Cucumber and Kidney Bean Salad

Preparation time: 10 minutes
Cooking time: 0 minutes
Servings: 4
Ingredients:
- 3 cups diced cucumber
- 1 (15-ounce / 425-g) can low-sodium dark red kidney beans, drained and rinsed
- 2 avocados, diced
- 1 1/2 cups diced tomatoes
- 1 cup cooked corn
- 3/4 cup sliced red onion
- 1 tablespoon extra-virgin olive oil
- 1 tablespoon apple cider vinegar

Directions:
1. In a large bowl, combine the cucumber, kidney beans, avocados, tomatoes, corn, onion, olive oil, and vinegar.

Nutrition:
- Calories: 320
- Fat: 16.1 g
- Protein: 10.1 g
- Carbohydrates: 35.9 g
- Fiber: 14.1 g
- Sugar: 7.0 g

124. Spinach and Chicken Salad

Preparation time: 5 minutes
Cooking time: 0 minutes
Servings: 4
Ingredients:
For the Salad:
- 8 cups baby spinach
- 2 cups shredded rotisserie chicken
- 1/2 cup sliced strawberries or other berries
- 1/2 cup sliced almonds
- 1 avocado, sliced
- 1/4 cup crumbled feta (optional)

For the Dressing:
- 2 tablespoons extra-virgin olive oil
- 2 teaspoons honey
- 2 teaspoons balsamic vinegar

Directions:
To Make the Salad
1. In a large bowl, combine the spinach, chicken, strawberries, and almonds.
2. Pour the dressing over the salad and lightly toss.
3. Divide into four equal portions and top each with sliced avocado and 1 tablespoon of crumbled feta (if using).

To Make the Dressing
1. In a small bowl, whisk together the olive oil, honey, and balsamic vinegar.

Nutrition:
- Calories: 340
- Fat: 22.1 g
- Protein: 25.1 g
- Carbohydrates: 12.9 g
- Fiber: 6.1 g
- Sugar: 6.0 g

125. Kale, Cantaloupe, and Chicken Salad

Preparation time: 10 minutes
Cooking time: 0 minutes
Servings: 3
Ingredients:
For the Salad:
- 4 cups chopped kale, packed
- 1 1/2 cups diced cantaloupe
- 1 1/2 cups shredded rotisserie chicken
- 1/2 cup sliced almonds
- 1/4 cup crumbled feta

For the Dressing:
- 2 teaspoons honey
- 2 tablespoons extra-virgin olive oil
- 2 teaspoons apple cider vinegar or freshly squeezed lemon juice

Directions:

To Make the Salad
1. Divide the kale into three portions. Layer 1/3 of the cantaloupe, chicken, almonds, and feta on each portion.
2. Drizzle some of the dressing over each portion of the salad. Serve immediately.

To Make the Dressing
1. In a small bowl, whisk together the honey, olive oil, and vinegar.

Nutrition:
- Calories: 395
- Fat: 22.1 g
- Protein: 27.1 g
- Carbohydrates: 23.9 g
- Fiber: 4.1 g
- Sugar: 12.0 g

126. Cobb Salad

Preparation time: 10 minutes
Cooking time: 30 minutes
Servings: 4
Ingredients:

For the Salad:
- 8 (2-ounce / 57-g) chicken tenders
- Avocado oil cooking spray
- 2 slices turkey bacon
- 2 (9-ounce / 255-g) packages shaved Brussels sprouts
- 2 hardboiled eggs, chopped
- 1/2 cup unsweetened dried cranberries

For the Dressing:
- 3 tablespoons honey mustard
- 3 tablespoons extra-virgin olive oil
- 1/2 tablespoon freshly squeezed lemon juice

Directions:

To Make the Salad
1. Preheat the oven to 425°F (220°C).
2. Lightly coat the chicken tenders with cooking spray, then place them on a baking sheet and bake for 15 to 18 minutes.
3. Meanwhile, heat a large skillet over medium-low heat. When hot, fry the bacon for 5 to 7 minutes until crispy. When the bacon is done, carefully remove it from the pan, and set it on a plate lined with a paper towel to drain and cool. Crumble when cool enough to handle.
4. Cut the chicken tenders into even pieces. Divide the Brussels sprouts into four equal portions. Top each portion with one-quarter of the chopped eggs, crumbled bacon, dried cranberries, and 2 sliced chicken tenders.
5. Drizzle an equal portion of dressing over each serving.

To Make the Dressing
1. In a small bowl, whisk together the mustard, olive oil, and lemon juice.

Nutrition:
- Calories: 467
- Fat: 20.1 g
- Protein: 35.1 g
- Carbohydrates: 36.9 g
- Fiber: 10.1 g
- Sugar: 14.0 g
- Sodium: 243 mg

127. Sofrito Steak and Veg Salad

Preparation time: 10 minutes
Cooking time: 15 minutes
Servings: 4
Ingredients:
- 4 ounces (113 g) recaíto cooking base
- 2 (4-ounce / 113-g) flank steaks
- 8 cups fresh spinach, loosely packed
- 1/2 cup sliced red onion
- 2 cups diced tomato
- 2 avocados, diced
- 2 cups diced cucumber
- 1/3 cup crumbled feta

Directions:
1. Heat a large skillet over medium-low heat. When hot, pour in the recaíto cooking base, add the steaks, and cover. Cook for 8 to 12 minutes.
2. Meanwhile, divide the spinach into four portions. Top each portion with one-quarter of the onion, tomato, avocados, and cucumber.

3. Remove the steak from the skillet, and let it rest for about 2 minutes before slicing. Place one-quarter of the steak and feta on top of each portion.

Nutrition:
- Calories: 346
- Fat: 18.1 g
- Protein: 25.1 g
- Carbohydrates: 17.9 g
- Fiber: 8.1 g
- Sugar: 6.0 g
- Sodium: 380 mg

128. Zucchini Salad with Ranch Dip

Preparation time: 10 minutes
Cooking time: 0 minutes
Servings: 4
Ingredients:
- 1 cup cottage cheese
- 2 tablespoons mayonnaise
- Juice of 1/2 lemon
- 2 tablespoons chopped fresh chives
- 2 tablespoons chopped fresh dill
- 2 scallions, white and green parts, finely chopped
- 1 garlic clove, minced
- 1/2 teaspoon sea salt
- 2 zucchinis, cut into sticks
- 8 cherry tomatoes

Directions:
1. In a small bowl, mix the cottage cheese, mayonnaise, lemon juice, chives, dill, scallions, garlic, and salt.
2. Serve with the zucchini sticks and cherry tomatoes for dipping.

Nutrition:
- Calories: 92
- Fat: 4.1 g
- Protein: 7.1 g
- Carbohydrates: 6.9 g
- Fiber: 1.1 g
- Sugar: 5.3 g
- Sodium: 388 mg

129. Spinach, Pear, and Walnut Salad

Preparation time: 10 minutes
Cooking time: 0 minutes
Servings: 2
Ingredients:
- 2 tablespoons apple cider vinegar
- 1 teaspoon peeled and grated fresh ginger
- 1/2 teaspoon Dijon mustard
- 2 tablespoons extra-virgin olive oil
- 1/2 teaspoon sea salt
- 4 cups baby spinach
- 1/2 pear, cored, peeled, and chopped
- 1/4 cup chopped walnuts

Directions:
1. Combine the vinegar, ginger, mustard, olive oil, and salt in a small bowl. Stir to mix well.
2. Combine the remaining ingredients in a large serving bowl, then toss to combine well.
3. Pour the vinegar dressing in the bowl of salad and toss before serving.

Nutrition:
- Calories: 229
- Fat: 20.4 g
- Protein: 3.5 g
- Carbohydrates: 10.7 g
- Fiber: 3.4 g
- Sugar: 4.9 g
- Sodium: 644 mg

130. Grain, Seafood, and Fruit Salad

Preparation time: 30 minutes
Cooking time: 20 minutes
Servings: 4
Ingredients:
- 1 cup quinoa, rinsed
- 1/2 pound (227 g) medium shrimps, peeled and deveined
- 1/2 pound (227 g) scallops
- 1 tablespoon olive oil
- 1/2 red bell pepper, chopped
- 1 roma plum tomatoes, deseeded and chopped
- 1 jalapeño pepper, stemmed and finely chopped
- 1/2 cup cooked black beans
- 1 mango, chopped
- 1 avocado, chopped

- 2 small scallions, chopped
- 2 tablespoons cilantro leaves, chopped

Citrus Dressing:
- 2 tablespoons lime juice
- 2 tablespoons orange juice
- 1 teaspoon honey
- 1/4 teaspoon cayenne pepper
- 1 tablespoon extra-virgin olive oil
- Sea salt, to taste

Directions:
1. Pour the quinoa in a pot, then pour in enough water to cover. Bring to a boil, then reduce the heat to low and simmer for 10 to 15 minutes or until the liquid has been absorbed. Fluff with a fork and let stand until ready to use.
2. Meanwhile, combine the ingredients for the citrus dressing in a small bowl. Stir to mix well. Set aside until ready to use.
3. Put the shrimps and scallops in a separate bowl, then drizzle with the olive oil. Toss to coat well.
4. Add the oiled shrimps and scallops in a nonstick skillet and grill over medium-high heat for 4 minutes or until opaque. Flip them halfway through. Remove them from the skillet and allow to cool.
5. Combine the cooked quinoa, shrimp and scallops with bell pepper, tomato, jalapeño, beans, mango, avocado, and scallions in a large salad bowl, then drizzle with the citrus dressing. Toss to combine well.
6. Garnish with cilantro leaves and serve immediately.

Nutrition:
- Calories: 470
- Fat: 16.0 g
- Protein: 30.0 g
- Carbohydrates: 56.0 g
- Fiber: 10.0 g
- Sugar: 16.0 g
- Sodium: 320 mg

131. Asian Noodle Salad

Preparation time: 30 minutes
Cooking time: 0 minutes
Servings: 4
Ingredients:
- 2 carrots, sliced thin
- 2 radish, sliced thin
- 1 English cucumber, sliced thin
- 1 mango, julienned
- 1 bell pepper, julienned
- 1 small serrano pepper, seeded and sliced thin
- 1 bag tofu Shirataki Fettuccini noodles
- 1/4 cup lime juice
- 1/4 cup fresh basil, chopped
- 1/4 cup fresh cilantro, chopped
- 2 tablespoons fresh mint, chopped
- 2 tablespoons rice vinegar
- 2 tablespoons sweet chili sauce
- 2 tablespoons roasted peanuts finely chopped
- 1 tablespoon Splenda
- 1/2 teaspoon sesame oil

Directions:
1. Pickle the vegetables: In a large bowl, place radish, cucumbers, and carrots. Add vinegar, coconut sugar, and lime juice and stir to coat the vegetables. Cover and chill 15 – 20 minutes.
2. Prep the noodles: remove the noodles from the package and rinse them under cold water. Cut into smaller pieces. Pat dry with paper towels.
3. To assemble the salad. Remove the vegetables from the marinade, reserving the marinade, and place in a large mixing bowl. Add noodles, mango, bell pepper, chili, and herbs.
4. In a small bowl, combine 2 tablespoons marinade with the chili sauce and sesame oil. Pour over salad and toss to coat. Top with peanuts and serve.

Nutrition:
- Calories: 159 Fat: 4.1 g
- Protein: 4.0 g Carbohydrates: 30.1 g
- Fiber: 6.1 g Sugar: 18.9 g Sodium: 119 mg

132. Cabbage Slaw Salad

Preparation time: 15 minutes
Cooking time: 0 minute
Servings: 4
Ingredients:
- 2 cups green cabbage
- 2 cups red cabbage

- 2 cups grated carrots
- 3 scallions
- 2 tablespoons extra-virgin olive oil
- 2 tablespoons rice vinegar
- 1 teaspoon honey
- 1 garlic clove
- 1/4 teaspoon salt

Directions:
1. Throw together the green and red cabbage, carrots, and scallions.
2. In a small bowl, whisk together the oil, vinegar, honey, garlic, and salt.
3. Pour the dressing over the veggies and mix to combine thoroughly.
4. Serve immediately, or cover and chill for several hours before serving.

Nutrition:
- Calories: 80
- Carbohydrates : 10 g
- Sugars : 6 g

133. Three Bean and Basil Salad

Preparation time: 10 minutes
Cooking time: 0 minute
Servings: 8
Ingredients:
- 1 (15-ounce) can low-sodium chickpeas
- 1 (15-ounce) can low-sodium kidney beans
- 1 (15-ounce) can low-sodium white beans
- 1 red bell pepper
- 1/4 cup chopped scallions
- 1/4 cup finely chopped fresh basil
- 3 garlic cloves, minced
- 2 tablespoons extra-virgin olive oil
- 1 tablespoon red wine vinegar
- 1 teaspoon Dijon mustard
- 1/4 teaspoon freshly ground black pepper

Directions:
1. Toss chickpeas, kidney beans, white beans, bell pepper, scallions, basil, and garlic gently.
2. Blend together olive oil, vinegar, mustard, and pepper. Toss with the salad.
3. Wrap and chill for 1 hour.

Nutrition:
- Calories 193
- Carbohydrates 29 g
- Sugars 3 g

134. Rainbow Black Bean Salad

Preparation time: 15 minutes
Cooking time: 0 minute
Servings: 5
Ingredients:
- 1 (15-ounce) can low-sodium black beans
- 1 avocado, diced
- 1 cup cherry
- tomatoes, halved
- 1 cup chopped baby spinach
- 1/2 cup red bell pepper
- 1/4 cup jicama
- 1/2 cup scallions
- 1/4 cup fresh cilantro
- 2 tablespoons lime juice
- 1 tablespoon extra-virgin olive oil
- 2 garlic cloves, minced
- 1 teaspoon honey
- 1/4 teaspoon salt
- 1/4 teaspoon freshly ground black pepper

Directions:
1. Mix black beans, avocado, tomatoes, spinach, bell pepper, jicama, scallions, and cilantro.
2. Blend lime juice, oil, garlic, honey, salt, and pepper. Add to the salad and toss.
3. Chill for 1 hour before serving.

Nutrition:
- Calories 169
- Carbohydrates 22 g
- Sugars 3 g

135. Warm Barley and Squash Salad

Preparation time: 20 minutes
Cooking time: 40 minutes
Servings: 8
Ingredients:
- 1 small butternut squash
- 3 tablespoons extra-virgin olive oil
- 2 cups broccoli florets
- 1 cup pearl barley
- 1 cup toasted chopped walnuts
- 2 cups baby kale
- 1/2 red onion, sliced
- 2 tablespoons balsamic vinegar
- 2 garlic cloves, minced
- 1/2 teaspoon salt

- 1/4 teaspoon black pepper

Directions:
1. Preheat the oven to 400°F. Line a baking sheet with parchment paper.
2. Peel off the squash, and slice into dice. In a large bowl, toss the squash with 2 teaspoons of olive oil. Transfer to the prepared baking sheet and roast for 20 minutes.
3. While the squash is roasting toss the broccoli in the same bowl with 1 teaspoon of olive oil. After 20 minutes, flip the squash and push it to one side of the baking sheet. Add the broccoli to the other side and continue to roast for 20 more minutes until tender.
4. While the veggies are roasting in a medium pot, cover the barley with several inches of water. Boil, then adjust heat, cover, and simmer for 30 minutes until tender. Drain and rinse.
5. Transfer the barley to a large bowl, and toss with the cooked squash and broccoli, walnuts, kale, and onion.
6. In a small bowl, mix the remaining 2 tablespoons of olive oil, balsamic vinegar, garlic, salt, and pepper. Drizzle dressing over the salad and toss.

Nutrition:
- Calories 274 Carbohydrates 32 g
- Sugars 3 g

136. Winter Chicken and Citrus Salad

Preparation time: 10 minutes
Cooking time: 0 minute
Servings: 4
Ingredients:
- 4 cups baby spinach
- 2 tablespoons extra-virgin olive oil
- 1 tablespoon lemon juice
- 1/8 teaspoon salt
- 2 cups chopped cooked chicken
- 2 mandarin oranges
- 1/2 peeled grapefruit, sectioned
- 1/4 cup sliced almonds

Directions:
1. Toss spinach with the olive oil, lemon juice, salt, and pepper.
2. Add the chicken, oranges, grapefruit, and almonds to the bowl. Toss gently.
3. Arrange on 4 plates and serve.

Nutrition:
- Calories 249
- Carbohydrates 11 g
- Sugars 7 g

137. Blueberry and Chicken Salad

Preparation time: 10 minutes
Cooking time: 0 minute
Servings: 4
Ingredients:
- 2 cups chopped cooked chicken
- 1 cup fresh blueberries
- 1/4 cup almonds
- 1 celery stalk
- 1/4 cup red onion
- 1 tablespoon fresh basil
- 1 tablespoon fresh cilantro
- 1/2 cup plain, vegan mayonnaise
- 1/4 teaspoon salt
- 1/4 teaspoon freshly ground black pepper
- 8 cups salad greens

Directions:
1. Toss chicken, blueberries, almonds, celery, onion, basil, and cilantro.
2. Blend yogurt, salt, and pepper. Stir chicken salad to combine.
3. Situate 2 cups of salad greens on each of 4 plates and divide the chicken salad among the plates to serve.

Nutrition:
- Calories 207
- Carbohydrates 11 g
- Sugars 6 g

138. Buffalo Chicken Salads

Preparation time: 7 minutes
Cooking time: 3 hours
Servings: 5
Ingredients:
- 1 ½ pound chicken breast halves
- 1/2 cup Wing Time Buffalo chicken sauce
- 4 teaspoons cider vinegar
- 1 teaspoon Worcestershire sauce
- 1 teaspoon paprika
- 1/3 cup light mayonnaise
- 2 tablespoons fat-free milk
- 2 tablespoons crumbled blue cheese

- 2 romaine hearts, chopped
- 1 cup whole grain croutons
- 1/2 cup very thinly sliced red onion

Directions:
1. Place chicken in a 2-quarts slow cooker. Mix together Worcestershire sauce, 2 teaspoons of vinegar and Buffalo sauce in a small bowl; pour over chicken. Dust with paprika. Close and cook for 3 hours on low-heat setting.
2. Mix the leftover 2 teaspoons of vinegar with milk and light mayonnaise together in a small bowl at serving time; mix in blue cheese. While chicken is still in the slow cooker, pull meat into bite-sized pieces using two forks.
3. Split the romaine among 6 dishes. Spoon sauce and chicken over lettuce. Pour with blue cheese dressing then add red onion slices and croutons on top.

Nutrition:
- Calories: 274
- Carbohydrate: 11 g
- Fiber: 2 g

139. Wild Rice Salad with Cranberries and Almonds

Preparation time: 6 minutes
Cooking time: 25 minutes
Servings: 18
Ingredients:
For the rice:
- 2 cups wild rice blend, rinsed
- 1 teaspoon kosher salt
- 2 1/2 cups Vegetable Broth

For the dressing:
- 1/4 cup extra-virgin olive oil
- 1/4 cup white wine vinegar
- 1 ½ teaspoon grated orange zest
- Juice of 1 medium orange (about 1/4 cup)
- 1 teaspoon honey or pure maple syrup

For the salad:
- 3/4 cup unsweetened dried cranberries
- 1/2 cup sliced almonds, toasted
- Freshly ground black pepper

Directions:
1. To make the rice
2. In the electric pressure cooker, combine the rice, salt, and broth.
3. Close and lock the lid. Set the valve to sealing.
4. Cook on high pressure for 25 minutes.
5. When the cooking is complete, hit Cancel and allow the pressure to release naturally for 1 minutes, then quick release any remaining pressure.
6. Once the pin drops, unlock and remove the lid.
7. Let the rice cool briefly, then fluff it with a fork.
8. To make the dressing
9. While the rice cooks, make the dressing: In a small jar with a screw-top lid, combine the olive oil, vinegar, zest, juice, and honey. (If you don't have a jar, whisk the ingredients together in a small bowl.) Shake to combine.
10. To make the salad
11. Mix rice, cranberries, and almonds.
12. Add the dressing and season with pepper.
13. Serve warm or refrigerate.

Nutrition:
- Calories: 126
- Carbohydrates: 18 g
- Fiber: 2 g

CHAPTER 10:

Soups and Stews Recipes

140. Authentic Gazpacho

Preparation time: 15 minutes
Cooking time: 0 minutes
Servings: 4
Ingredients:
- 3 pounds (1.4 kg) ripe tomatoes, chopped
- 1 cup low-sodium tomato juice
- 1/2 red onion, chopped
- 1 cucumber, peeled, seeded, and chopped
- 1 red bell pepper, seeded and chopped
- 2 celery stalks, chopped
- 2 tablespoons chopped fresh parsley
- 2 garlic cloves, chopped
- 2 tablespoons extra-virgin olive oil
- 2 tablespoons red wine vinegar
- 1 teaspoon honey
- 1/2 teaspoon salt
- 1/4 teaspoon freshly ground black pepper

Directions:
1. In a blender jar, combine the tomatoes, tomato juice, onion, cucumber, bell pepper, celery, parsley, garlic, olive oil, vinegar, honey, salt, and pepper. Pulse until blended but still slightly chunky.
2. Adjust the seasonings as needed and serve.
3. To store, transfer to a nonreactive, airtight container and refrigerate for up to 3 days.

Nutrition:
- Calories: 170
- Fat: 8 g
- Protein: 5 g
- Carbohydrates: 24 g
- Sugars: 16 g
- Fiber: 6 g
- Sodium: 332 mg

141. Tomato Kale Soup

Preparation time: 10 minutes
Cooking time: 15 minutes
Servings: 4
Ingredients:
- 1 tablespoon extra-virgin olive oil
- 1 medium onion, chopped
- 2 carrots, finely chopped
- 3 garlic cloves, minced
- 4 cups low-sodium vegetable broth
- 1 (28-ounce / 794-g) can crushed tomatoes
- 1/2 teaspoon dried oregano
- 1/4 teaspoon dried basil
- 4 cups chopped baby kale leaves
- 1/4 teaspoon salt

Directions:
1. In a large pot, heat the oil over medium heat. Add the onion and carrots to the pan. Sauté for 3 to 5 minutes until they begin to soften. Add the garlic and sauté for 30 seconds more, until fragrant.
2. Add the vegetable broth, tomatoes, oregano, and basil to the pot and bring to a boil. Reduce the heat to low and simmer for 5 minutes.
3. Using an immersion blender, purée the soup.
4. Add the kale and simmer for 3 more minutes. Season with the salt. Serve immediately.

Nutrition:
- Calories: 172
- Fat: 5 g
- Protein: 6 g
- Carbohydrates: 30 g
- Sugars: 13 g
- Fiber: 8 g
- Sodium: 601 mg

142. Zucchini Soup with Roasted Chickpeas

Preparation time: 10 minutes
Cooking time: 20 minutes
Servings: 4
Ingredients:
- 1 (15-ounce / 425-g) can low-sodium chickpeas, drained and rinsed
- 1 teaspoon extra-virgin olive oil, plus 1 tablespoon
- 1/4 teaspoon smoked paprika
- Pinch salt, plus 1/2 teaspoon
- 3 medium zucchini, coarsely chopped
- 3 cups low-sodium vegetable broth
- 1/2 onion, diced
- 3 garlic cloves, minced
- 2 tablespoons plain low-fat Greek yogurt
- Freshly ground black pepper, to taste

Directions:
1. Preheat the oven to 425°F (220°C). Line a baking sheet with parchment paper.
2. In a medium mixing bowl, toss the chickpeas with 1 teaspoon of olive oil, the smoked paprika, and a pinch salt. Transfer to the prepared baking sheet and roast until crispy, about 20 minutes, stirring once. Set aside.
3. Meanwhile, in a medium pot, heat the remaining 1 tablespoon of oil over medium heat.
4. Add the zucchini, broth, onion, and garlic to the pot, and bring to a boil. Reduce the heat to a simmer, and cook until the zucchini and onion are tender, about 20 minutes.
5. In a blender jar, or using an immersion blender, purée the soup. Return to the pot.
6. Add the yogurt, remaining 1/2 teaspoon of salt, and pepper, and stir well. Serve topped with the roasted chickpeas.

Nutrition:
- Calories: 189
- Fat: 7 g
- Protein: 8 g
- Carbohydrates: 24 g
- Sugars: 7 g
- Fiber: 7 g
- Sodium: 527 mg

143. Thai Shrimp Soup

Preparation time: 10 minutes
Cooking time: 10 minutes
Servings: 4
Ingredients:
- 1 tablespoon coconut oil
- 1 tablespoon Thai red curry paste
- 1/2 onion, sliced
- 3 garlic cloves, minced
- 2 cups chopped carrots
- 1/2 cup whole unsalted peanuts
- 4 cups low-sodium vegetable broth
- 1/2 cup unsweetened plain almond milk
- 1/2 pound (227 g) shrimp, peeled and deveined
- Minced fresh cilantro, for garnish

Directions:
1. In a large pan, heat the oil over medium-high heat until shimmering.
2. Add the curry paste and cook, stirring constantly, for 1 minute. Add the onion, garlic, carrots, and peanuts to the pan, and continue to cook for 2 to 3 minutes until the onion begins to soften.
3. Add the broth and bring to a boil. Reduce the heat to low and simmer for 5 to 6 minutes until the carrots are tender.
4. Using an immersion blender or in a blender, purée the soup until smooth and return it to the pot. With the heat still on low, add the almond milk and stir to combine. Add the shrimp to the pot and cook for 2 to 3 minutes until cooked through.
5. Garnish with cilantro and serve.

Nutrition:
- Calories: 237
- Fat: 14 g
- Protein: 14 g
- Carbohydrates: 17 g
- Sugars: 6 g
- Fiber: 5 g
- Sodium: 619 mg

144. Lime Chicken Tortilla Soup

Preparation time: 10 minutes
Cooking time: 35 minutes
Servings: 4
Ingredients:
- 1 tablespoon extra-virgin olive oil
- 1 onion, thinly sliced
- 1 garlic clove, minced
- 1 jalapeño pepper, diced
- 2 boneless, skinless chicken breasts
- 4 cups low-sodium chicken broth
- 1 Roma tomato, diced
- 1/2 teaspoon salt
- 2 (6-inch) corn tortillas, cut into thin strips
- Nonstick cooking spray
- Juice of 1 lime
- Minced fresh cilantro, for garnish
- 1/4 cup shredded Cheddar cheese, for garnish

Directions:
1. In a medium pot, heat the oil over medium-high heat. Add the onion and cook for 3 to 5 minutes until it begins to soften. Add the

garlic and jalapeño, and cook until fragrant, about 1 minute more.
2. Add the chicken, chicken broth, tomato, and salt to the pot and bring to a boil. Reduce the heat to medium and simmer gently for 20 to 25 minutes until the chicken breasts are cooked through. Remove the chicken from the pot and set aside.
3. Preheat a broiler to high.
4. Spray the tortilla strips with nonstick cooking spray and toss to coat. Spread in a single layer on a baking sheet and broil for 3 to 5 minutes, flipping once, until crisp.
5. When the chicken is cool enough to handle, shred it with two forks and return to the pot.
6. Season the soup with the lime juice. Serve hot, garnished with cilantro, cheese, and tortilla strips.

Nutrition:
- Calories: 191
- Fat: 8 g
- Protein: 19 g
- Carbohydrates: 13 g
- Sugars: 2 g
- Fiber: 2 g
- Sodium: 482 mg

145. Split Pea Soup with Carrots

Preparation time: 8 minutes
Cooking time: 15 minutes
Servings: 4
Ingredients:
- 1 1/2 cups dried green split peas, rinsed and drained
- 4 cups vegetable broth or water
- 2 celery stalks, chopped
- 1 medium onion, chopped
- 2 carrots, chopped
- 3 garlic cloves, minced
- 1 teaspoon herbes de Provence
- 1 teaspoon liquid smoke
- Kosher salt and freshly ground black pepper, to taste
- Shredded carrot, for garnish (optional)

Directions:
1. In the electric pressure cooker, combine the peas, broth, celery, onion, carrots, garlic, herbes de Provence, and liquid smoke.
2. Close and lock the lid of the pressure cooker. Set the valve to sealing.
3. Cook on high pressure for 15 minutes.
4. When the cooking is complete, hit Cancel and allow the pressure to release naturally for 10 minutes, then quick release any remaining pressure.
5. Once the pin drops, unlock and remove the lid.
6. Stir the soup and season with salt and pepper.
7. Spoon into serving bowls and sprinkle shredded carrots on top (if using).

Nutrition:
- Calories: 284
- Fat: 1 g
- Protein: 19 g
- Carbohydrates: 52 g
- Sugars: 9 g
- Fiber: 21 g
- Sodium: 60 mg

146. Moroccan Eggplant Stew

Preparation time: 20 minutes
Cooking time: 3 minutes
Servings: 4
Ingredients:
- 2 tablespoons avocado oil
- 1 large onion, minced
- 2 garlic cloves, minced
- 1 teaspoon ras el hanout spice blend or curry powder
- 1/4 teaspoon cayenne pepper
- 1 teaspoon kosher salt
- 1 cup vegetable broth or water
- 1 tablespoon tomato paste
- 2 cups chopped eggplant
- 2 medium gold potatoes, peeled and chopped
- 4 ounces (113 g) tomatillos, husks removed, chopped
- 1 (14-ounce / 397-g) can diced tomatoes

Directions:
1. Set the electric pressure cooker to the Sauté setting. When the pot is hot, pour in the avocado oil.
2. Sauté the onion for 3 to 5 minutes, until it begins to soften. Add the garlic, ras el

hanout, cayenne, and salt. Cook and stir for about 30 seconds. Hit Cancel.
3. Stir in the broth and tomato paste. Add the eggplant, potatoes, tomatillos, and tomatoes with their juices.
4. Close and lock the lid of the pressure cooker. Set the valve to sealing.
5. Cook on high pressure for 3 minutes.
6. When the cooking is complete, hit Cancel and allow the pressure to release naturally.
7. Once the pin drops, unlock and remove the lid.
8. Stir well and spoon into serving bowls.

Nutrition:
- Calories: 216
- Fat: 8 g
- Protein: 4 g
- Carbohydrates: 28 g
- Sugars: 9 g
- Fiber: 8 g
- Sodium: 735 mg

147. Cheeseburger Soup

Preparation time: 5 minutes
Cooking time: 25 minutes
Servings: 4
Ingredients:
- Avocado oil cooking spray
- 1/2 cup diced white onion
- 1/2 cup diced celery
- 1/2 cup sliced portobello mushrooms
- 1 pound (454 g) 93% lean ground beef
- 1 (15-ounce / 425-g) can no-salt-added diced tomatoes
- 2 cups low-sodium beef broth
- 1/3 cup half-and-half
- 3/4 cup shredded sharp Cheddar cheese

Directions:
1. Heat a large stockpot over medium-low heat. When hot, coat the cooking surface with cooking spray. Put the onion, celery, and mushrooms into the pot. Cook for 7 minutes, stirring occasionally.
2. Add the ground beef and cook for 5 minutes, stirring and breaking apart as needed.
3. Add the diced tomatoes with their juices and the broth. Increase the heat to medium-high and simmer for 10 minutes.
4. Remove the pot from the heat and stir in the half-and-half.
5. Serve topped with the cheese.

Nutrition:
- Calories: 330 Fat: 18 g
- Protein: 33 g Carbohydrates: 9 g
- Sugars: 5 g Fiber: 2 g Sodium: 321 mg

148. Taco Soup

Preparation time: 5 minutes
Cooking time: 20 minutes
Servings: 4
Ingredients:
- Avocado oil cooking spray
- 1 medium red bell pepper, chopped
- 1/2 cup chopped yellow onion
- 1 pound (454 g) 93% lean ground beef
- 1 teaspoon ground cumin
- 1/2 teaspoon salt
- 1/2 teaspoon chili powder
- 1/2 teaspoon garlic powder
- 2 cups low-sodium beef broth
- 1 (15-ounce / 425-g) can no-salt-added diced tomatoes
- 1 ½ cup frozen corn
- 1/3 cup half-and-half

Directions:
1. Heat a large stockpot over medium-low heat. When hot, coat the cooking surface with cooking spray. Put the pepper and onion in the pan and cook for 5 minutes.
2. Add the ground beef, cumin, salt, chili powder, and garlic powder. Cook for 5 to 7 minutes, stirring and breaking apart the beef as needed.
3. Add the broth, diced tomatoes with their juices, and corn. Increase the heat to medium-high and simmer for 10 minutes.
4. Remove from the heat and stir in the half-and-half.

Nutrition:
- Calories: 320
- Fat: 12 g Protein: 30 g
- Carbohydrates: 23 g
- Sugars: 7 g
- Fiber: 4 g
- Sodium: 456 mg

149. Lentil Vegetable Soup

Preparation time: 10 minutes
Cooking time: 15 minutes
Servings: 4
Ingredients:
- 2 tablespoons extra-virgin olive oil
- 1 onion, finely chopped
- 1 carrot, chopped
- 1 cup chopped kale (stems removed)
- 3 garlic cloves, minced
- 1 cup canned lentils, drained and rinsed
- 5 cups unsalted vegetable broth
- 2 teaspoons dried rosemary (or 1 tablespoon chopped fresh rosemary)
- 1/2 teaspoon sea salt
- 1/4 teaspoon freshly ground black pepper

Directions:
1. In a large pot over medium-high heat, heat the olive oil until it shimmers. Add the onion and carrot and cook, stirring until the vegetables begin to soften, about 3 minutes. Add the kale and cook for 3 minutes more. Add the garlic and cook, stirring constantly, for 30 seconds.
2. Stir in the lentils, vegetable broth, rosemary, salt, and pepper. Bring to a simmer. Simmer, stirring occasionally, for 5 minutes more.

Nutrition:
- Calories: 160
- Fat: 7 g Protein: 6 g
- Carbohydrates: 19 g
- Sugars: 12 g
- Fiber: 6 g
- Sodium: 187 mg

150. Quick Clam Chowder

Preparation time: 10 minutes
Cooking time: 15 minutes
Servings: 4
Ingredients:
- 2 tablespoons extra-virgin olive oil
- 3 slices pepper bacon, chopped
- 1 onion, chopped
- 1 red bell pepper, seeded and chopped
- 1 fennel bulb, chopped
- 3 tablespoons flour
- 5 cups low-sodium or unsalted chicken broth
- 6 ounces (170 g) chopped canned clams, undrained
- 1/2 teaspoon sea salt
- 1/2 cup milk

Directions:
1. In a large pot over medium-high heat, heat the olive oil until it shimmers. Add the bacon and cook, stirring until browned, about 4 minutes. Remove the bacon from the fat with a slotted spoon, and set it aside on a plate.
2. Add the onion, bell pepper, and fennel to the fat in the pot. Cook, stirring occasionally, until the vegetables are soft, about 5 minutes. Add the flour and cook, stirring constantly, for 1 minute. Add the broth, clams, and salt. Bring to a simmer. Cook, stirring until the soup thickens, about 5 minutes more.
3. Stir in the milk and return the bacon to the pot. Cook, stirring 1 minute more.

Nutrition:
- Calories: 335
- Fat: 20 g
- Protein: 20 g
- Carbohydrates: 21 g
- Sugars: 6 g
- Fiber: 3 g
- Sodium: 496 mg

151. Beef Barley Soup

Preparation time: 20 minutes
Cooking time: 30 minutes
Servings: 4
Ingredients:
- 2 teaspoons extra-virgin olive oil
- 1 sweet onion, chopped
- 1 tablespoon minced garlic
- 4 celery stalks, with greens, chopped
- 2 carrots, peeled, diced
- 1 sweet potato, peeled, diced
- 8 cups low-sodium beef broth
- 1 cup cooked pearl barley
- 2 cups diced cooked beef
- 2 bay leaves
- 2 teaspoons hot sauce
- 2 teaspoons chopped fresh thyme

- 1 cup shredded kale
- Sea salt and freshly ground black pepper, to taste

Directions:
1. Place a large stockpot over medium-high heat and add the oil.
2. Sauté the onion and garlic until softened and translucent, about 3 minutes.
3. Stir in the celery, carrot, and sweet potato, and sauté for a further 5 minutes.
4. Stir in the beef broth, barley, beef, bay leaves, and hot sauce.
5. Bring the soup to a boil, then reduce the heat to low.
6. Simmer until the vegetables are tender, about 15 minutes.
7. Remove the bay leaves and stir in the thyme and kale.
8. Simmer for 5 minutes, and season with salt and pepper.

Nutrition:
- Calories: 345
- Fat: 11 g
- Protein: 28 g
- Carbohydrates: 33 g
- Sugars: 8 g
- Fiber: 5 g
- Sodium: 837 mg

152. Creamy Chicken Soup

Preparation time: 35 min
Cooking time: 30 minutes
Servings: 4
Ingredients:
- 4 chicken breasts
- 1 carrot, chopped
- 1 cup zucchini, peeled and chopped
- 2 cups cauliflower, broken into florets
- 1 celery rib, chopped
- 1 small onion, chopped
- 5 cups water
- 1/2 tsp salt
- black pepper, to taste

Directions:
1. Place chicken breasts, onion, carrot, celery, cauliflower and zucchini in a deep soup pot. Add in salt, black pepper and 5 cups of water. Stir and bring to a boil.
2. Simmer for 30 minutes then remove chicken from the pot and let it cool slightly.
3. Blend soup until completely smooth. Shred or dice the chicken meat, return it back to the pot, stir, and serve.

Nutrition:
- Calories: 557 Fat: 28.44 g
- Protein: 66.22 g Carbohydrates: 5.84 g
- Fiber: 1.8 g Sodium: 516 mg

153. Broccoli and Chicken Soup

Preparation time: 35 min
Cooking time: 30 minutes
Servings: 4
Ingredients:
- 4 boneless chicken thighs, diced
- 1 small carrot, chopped
- 1 broccoli head, broken into florets
- 1 garlic clove, chopped
- 1 small onion, chopped
- 4 cups water
- 3 tbsp extra virgin olive oil
- 1/2 tsp salt
- black pepper, to taste

Directions:
1. In a deep soup pot, heat olive oil and gently sauté broccoli for 2-3 minutes, stirring occasionally. Add in onion, carrot, chicken and cook, stirring for 2-3 minutes. Stir in salt, black pepper and water.
2. Bring to a boil. Simmer for 30 minutes then remove from heat and set aside to cool.
3. In a blender or food processor, blend soup until completely smooth. Serve and enjoy!

Nutrition:
- Calories: 498
- Fat: 34.41 g
- Protein: 25.22 g
- Carbohydrates: 22.01 g
- Fiber: 0.7 g
- Sodium: 1476 mg

154. Guinness Beef Stew with Cauliflower Mash

Preparation time: 10 minutes
Cooking time: 8 hours
Servings: 4
Ingredients:
- 2 pounds (907 g) beef round steak, cut into 1-inch cubes
- 1 large head cauliflower, separated into florets
- 5 sprigs fresh thyme
- 1 medium carrot, cut into 1/2-inch pieces
- 1 stick of celery, cut into 1/2-inch pieces
- 1 cup yellow onion, cut into large pieces
- 2/3 cup Guinness
- 1 tablespoon margarine
- 2 cups low sodium beef broth
- 2 tablespoons arrowroot starch
- 1 tablespoon plus 1 teaspoon garlic, diced fine
- 2 teaspoons olive oil
- Sea salt and pepper to taste

Directions:
1. Add oil to a large nonstick skillet and heat over medium-high heat. Add beef and sear on all sides. Transfer to crock pot.
2. Add thyme, Guinness, carrot, onion, celery, garlic, and broth. Set to low and cook 6 to 8 hours, or 4 to 5 on high.
3. One hour before the stew is ready, mix arrowroot with 1 ½ tablespoon water and stir into stew.
4. For the mash: bring 2 cups water to a boil in a large pot and add cauliflower. Cover and cook 10 to 12 minutes, or until cauliflower is soft.
5. Drain. Add salt, pepper, 1 teaspoon garlic, and margarine. Use an immersion blender and process until it resembles mashed potatoes.
6. To serve: ladle stew in a bowl and spoon about 1/4 cup of the mash on top. Garnish with fresh thyme, parsley, and cracked pepper if desired.

Nutrition:
- Calories: 564
- Fat: 28.0 g
- Protein: 75.2 g
- Carbohydrates: 17.1 g
- Fiber: 5.9 g
- Sugar: 7.1 g

CHAPTER 11:

Snack Recipes

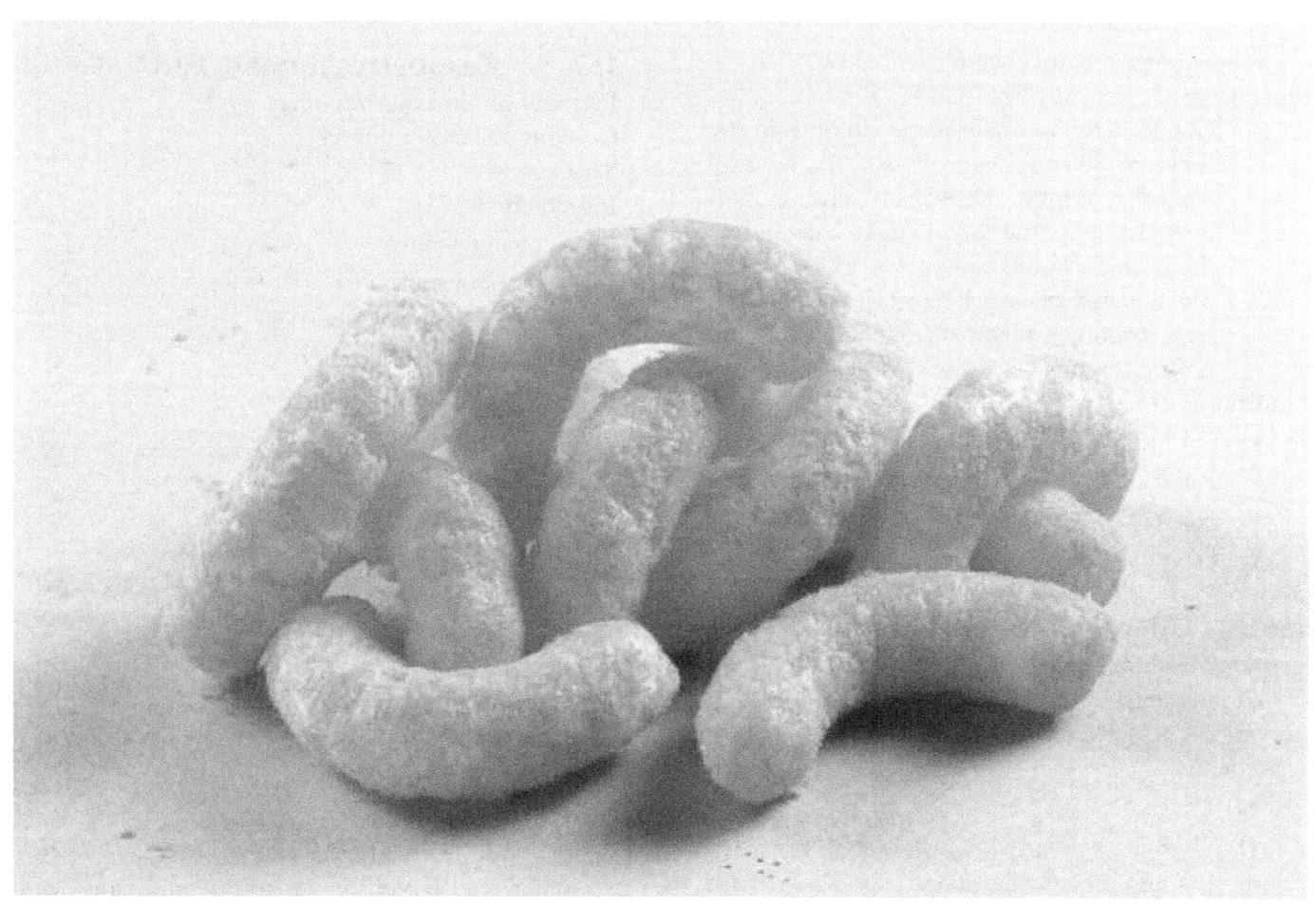

155. Mortadella & Bacon Balls

Preparation time: 10 minutes
Cooking time: 30 minutes
Servings: 2
Ingredients:
- 4 ounces Mortadella sausage
- 4 bacon slices, cooked and crumbled
- 2 tbsp almonds, chopped
- 1/2 tsp Dijon mustard
- 3 ounces' cream cheese

Directions:
1. Combine the mortadella and almonds in the bowl of your food processor. Pulse until smooth. Whisk the cream cheese and mustard in another bowl. Make balls out of the mortadella mixture.
2. Make a thin cream cheese layer over. Coat with bacon, arrange on a plate and chill before serving.

Nutrition:
- Calories 547
- Fat: 51 g
- Net Carbohydrates: 3.4 g
- Protein: 21.5 g

156. Crispy Baked Cheese Puffs

Preparation time: 5 minutes
Cooking time: 10 minutes
Servings: 4
Ingredients:
- 2 eggs
- 1/2 cup cheddar cheese, grated
- 1/4 cup mozzarella, grated

What you'll need from store cupboard:
- 1/2 cup almond flour
- 1/4 cup reduced fat Parmesan
- 1/2 tsp baking powder
- Black pepper

Directions:
1. Heat oven to 400 degrees. Line a baking sheet with parchment paper.
2. In a large bowl, whisk eggs until lightly beaten. Add remaining Ingredients and mix well.
3. Divide into 8 pieces and roll into balls. Place on prepared baking sheet. Bake 10-12 minutes or until golden brown. Serve as is or with your favorite dipping sauce.

Nutrition:
- Calories 129
- Total Carbs 2 g
- Net Carbs 1 g
- Protein 8 g
- Fat 10 g
- Sugar 0 g
- Fiber 1 g

157. Raspberry Almond Tart

Preparation time: 10 minutes
Cooking time: 30 minutes
Servings: 4
Ingredients:
- 5 egg whites
- 1 tsp vanilla
- 1 1/2 cups raspberries
- 1 lemon zest, grated
- 1 cup almond flour
- 1/2 cup Swerve
- 1/2 cup butter, melted
- 1 tsp baking powder

Directions:
1. Preheat the oven to 375° F/ 190° C.
2. Grease tart tin with cooking spray and set aside.
3. In a large bowl, whisk egg whites until foamy.
4. Add sweetener, baking powder, vanilla, lemon zest, and almond flour and mix until well combined.
5. Add melted butter and stir well.
6. Pour batter in tart tin and top with raspberries.
7. Bake in preheated oven for 20-23 minutes.
8. Serve and enjoy.

Nutrition:
- Calories 378
- Fat 8 g
- Carbohydrates 14 g
- Sugar 4 g
- Protein 11 g
- Cholesterol 0 mg

158. Oatmeal Butterscotch Cookies

Preparation time: 10 minutes
Cooking time: 30 minutes
Servings: 4
Ingredients:
- 1/2 teaspoon cinnamon, ground
- 3 cups oats
- 2 eggs

What you will need from the store cupboard:
- 1 teaspoon of baking soda
- 1-1/4 all-purpose flour
- 1 cup margarine or butter
- 1 teaspoon vanilla extract
- 1/2 teaspoon salt

Directions:
1. Preheat your oven to 350 °F.
2. Bring together the baking soda, flour, salt and cinnamon in a bowl.
3. Beat the eggs, vanilla extract and butter in a mixer bowl.
4. Beat in the flour mix gradually.
5. Stir in the oats.
6. Place rounded tablespoons on baking sheets. Bake for 5-6 minutes.
7. Let it cool for a couple of minutes.

Nutrition:
- Calories 130
- Carbohydrates 16 g
- Cholesterol 20 mg
- Fat 7 g
- Protein 1 g
- Sodium 90 mg

159. Quail Eggs & Prosciutto Wraps

Preparation time: 10 minutes
Cooking time: 30 minutes
Servings: 2
Ingredients:
- 3 thin prosciutto slices
- 9 basil leaves
- 9 quail eggs

Directions:
1. Cover the quail eggs with salted water and bring to a boil over medium heat for 2-3 minutes. Place the eggs in an ice bath and let cool for 10 minutes, then peel them.
2. Cut the prosciutto slices into three strips. Place basil leaves at the end of each strip. Top with a quail egg. Wrap in prosciutto, secure with toothpicks and serve.

Nutrition:
- Calories 243
- Fat: 21 g
- Net Carbohydrates: 0.5 g
- Protein: 12.5 g

160. Pumpkin Spiced Almonds

Preparation time: 10 minutes
Cooking time: 30 minutes
Servings: 4
Ingredients:
- 1 tablespoon olive oil
- 1 1/4 teaspoon pumpkin pie spice
- Pinch salt
- 1 cup whole almonds, raw

Directions:
1. Preheat the oven to 300°F and line a baking sheet with parchment.
2. Whisk together the olive oil, pumpkin pie spice, and salt in a mixing bowl.
3. Toss in the almonds until evenly coated, then spread on the baking sheet.
4. Bake for 25 minutes, then cool completely and store in an airtight container.

Nutrition:
- Calories 170
- Fat 15.5 g
- Protein 5 g
- Carbs 5.5 g
- Fiber 3 g
- Net carbs 2.5 g

161. Cheese Crisp Crackers

Preparation time: 10 minutes
Cooking time: 30 minutes
Servings: 4
Ingredients:
- 4 slices pepper Jack cheese, quartered
- 4 slices Colby Jack cheese, quartered
- 4 slices cheddar cheese, quartered

Directions:
1. Heat oven to 400 degrees. Line a cooking sheet with parchment paper.
2. Place cheese in a single layer on a prepared pan and bake 10 minutes, or until cheese gets firm.

3. Transfer to paper towel line surface to absorb excess oil. Let cool, cheese will crisp up more as it cools.
4. Store in an airtight container or Ziploc bag. Serve with your favorite dip or salsa.

Nutrition:
- Calories 253 Total Carbs 1 g
- Protein 15 g
- Fat 20 g
- Sugar 0 g
- Fiber 0 g

162. Tortilla Chips

Preparation time: 10 minutes
Cooking time: 30 minutes
Servings: 4
Ingredients:
- 2 cup part-skim grated mozzarella cheese, grated

What you'll need from store cupboard:
- 3/4 cup super fine almond flour
- 1/2 tsp salt
- 1/2 tsp chili powder

Directions:
1. Heat oven to 375° degrees.
2. Prepare a double boiler. Over high heat, bring the water in the pot to a simmer, then turn heat to low. Add all the Ingredients to the top of the double boiler and stir constantly until cheese melts and mixture holds together in a ball. Turn out onto a large piece of parchment paper and let cool 5 minutes.
3. Knead the dough to thoroughly combine all the Ingredients. Separate into 2 equal portions. Working with one portion at a time, roll the dough out between two pieces of parchment paper into 9x15-inch rectangle.
4. Remove top piece of parchment and with a pizza cutter, or sharp knife, cut rectangle into squares or triangles. Slide the parchment paper onto a cookie sheet and arrange dough shapes so they have 1/2-inch space between them. Repeat with second dough portion.
5. Bake 5-8 minutes, or until centers are golden brown. Remove from oven and transfer to a wire rack to cool. Chips will crisp up as they cool. Store in an airtight container.

Nutrition:
- Calories 95
- Total Carbs 3 g
- Net Carbs 2 g
- Protein 5 g
- Fat 8 g
- Sugar 0 g
- Fiber 1 g

163. Hot & Spicy Mixed Nuts

Preparation time: 10 Minutes
Cooking time: 40 minutes
Servings: 6
Ingredients:
What you'll need from store cupboard:
- 1/2 cup whole almonds
- 1/2 cup pecan halves
- 1/2 cup walnut halves
- 1 tsp sunflower oil
- 1/2 tsp cumin
- 1/2 tsp curry powder
- 1/8 tsp cayenne pepper
- Dash of white pepper

Directions:
1. Heat oven to 350°F.
2. Place the nuts in a large bowl. Add the oil and toss to coat.
3. Stir the spices together in a small bowl. Add to nuts and toss to coat.
4. Spread nuts on a large baking sheet in a single layer. Bake 10 minutes.
5. Remove from oven and let cool. Store in airtight container. Serving size is 1/4 cup.

Nutrition:
- Calories 257
- Total Carbs 5 g
- Net Carbs 1 g
- Protein 6 g
- Fat 25 g
- Sugar 1 g
- Fiber 4 g

164. Mozzarella Sticks

Preparation time: 10 Minutes
Cooking time: 40 minutes
Servings: 4
Ingredients:
- 8 string cheese sticks, halved

- 2 eggs, beaten

What you'll need from store cupboard:
- 1 cup reduced-fat parmesan cheese
- 1/2 cup sunflower oil
- 1 tbsp. Italian seasoning
- 1 clove garlic, diced fine

Directions:
1. Heat oil in a pot over med-high heat.
2. In a medium bowl, combine parmesan cheese, Italian seasoning and garlic.
3. In a small bowl, beat the eggs.
4. Dip string cheese in eggs then in parmesan mixture to coat, pressing coating into cheese.
5. Place in hot oil and cook until golden brown. Transfer to paper towel lined plate. Serve warm with marinara sauce.

Nutrition:
- Calories 290
- Total Carbs 3 g
- Protein 24 g
- Fat 20 g
- Sugar 0 g
- Fiber 0 g

165. Buffalo Bites

Preparation time: 10 Minutes
Cooking time: 40 minutes
Servings: 4
Ingredients:
- 1 egg
- 1/2 head of cauliflower, separated into florets

What you'll need from store cupboard:
- 1 cup panko bread crumbs
- 1 cup low-fat ranch dressing
- 1/2 cup hot sauce
- 1/2 tsp salt
- 1/2 tsp garlic powder
- Black pepper
- Nonstick cooking spray

Directions:
1. Heat oven to 400 degrees. Spray a baking sheet with cooking spray.
2. Place the egg in a medium bowl and mix in the salt, pepper and garlic. Place the panko crumbs into a small bowl.
3. Dip the florets first in the egg then into the panko crumbs. Place in a single layer on prepared pan.
4. Bake 8-10 minutes, stirring halfway through, until cauliflower is golden brown and crisp on the outside.
5. In a small bowl, stir the dressing and hot sauce together. Use for dipping.

Nutrition:
- Calories 132
- Total Carbs 15 g
- Net Carbs 14 g
- Protein 6 g
- Fat 5 g
- Sugar 4 g
- Fiber 1 g

166. Plum & Pistachio Snack

Preparation time: 10 minutes
Cooking time: 30 minutes
Servings: 1
Ingredients:
- 1/4 cup unsalted dry-roasted pistachios (measured in shell)
- 1 plum

Directions:
1. Hull and serve pistachios together with plum.

Nutrition:
- Calories: 113 calories;
- Total Carbohydrate: 12 g
- Cholesterol: 0 mg
- Total Fat: 7 g
- Fiber: 2 g
- Protein: 4 g
- Sodium: 1 mg
- Sugar: 8 g
- Saturated Fat: 1 g

167. Avocado and Tempeh Bacon Wraps

Preparation time: 10 minutes
Cooking time: 30 minutes
Servings: 4
Ingredients:
- 2 tablespoons extra-virgin olive oil
- 8 ounces tempeh bacon, homemade or store-bought

- 4 (10-inch) soft flour tortillas or lavish flat bread
- 1/4 cup vegan mayonnaise, homemade or store-bought
- 4 large lettuce leaves
- 2 ripe Hass avocados, pitted, peeled, and cut into 1/4-inch slices
- 1 large ripe tomato, cut into 1/4-inch slices

Directions:
1. Cook the tempeh bacon until browned on both sides in a large skillet about 8 minutes. Remove from the heat and set aside.
2. Place 1 tortilla on a work surface. Spread with some of the mayonnaise and one-fourth of the lettuce and tomatoes.
3. Finish and Serve
4. Pit, peel, and thinly slice the avocado and place the slices on top of the tomato. Add the reserved tempeh bacon and roll up tightly. Repeat with remaining Ingredients and serve.

Nutrition:
- Fat: 24.3 g
- Protein: 11.7 g
- Carbohydrates: 16.7 g

168. Cinnamon Apple Chips

Preparation time: 5 minutes
Cooking time: 10 minutes
Servings: 2
Ingredients:
- 1 medium apple, sliced thin

What you'll need from store cupboard:
- 1/4 tsp cinnamon
- 1/4 tsp nutmeg
- Nonstick cooking spray

Directions:
1. Heat oven to 375°F. Spray a baking sheet with cooking spray.
2. Place apples in a mixing bowl and add spices. Toss to coat.
3. Arrange apples, in a single layer, on prepared pan. Bake 4 minutes, turn apples over and bake 4 minutes more.
4. Serve immediately or store in an airtight container.

Nutrition:
- Calories 58
- Total Carbs 15 g
- Protein 0 g
- Fat 0 g
- Sugar 11 g
- Fiber 3 g

169. Tofu & Chia Seed Pudding

Preparation time: 10 minutes
Cooking time: 30 minutes
Servings: 4
Ingredients:
- 1-pound silken tofu, pressed and drained
- 1/4 cup banana, peeled
- 3 tablespoons cacao powder
- 1 teaspoon vanilla extract
- 3 tablespoons chia seeds
- 1/4 cup walnuts, chopped
- 1/4 cup black raisins

Directions:
1. In a food processor, add tofu, banana, cocoa powder, and vanilla, and pulse till smooth and creamy.
2. Transfer into a large serving bowl and stir in chia seeds till well mixed.
3. Now, place the pudding in serving bowls evenly.
4. With plastic wraps, cover the bowls. Refrigerate to chill before serving.
5. Garnish with raspberries and serve.

Nutrition:
- Calories 188
- Total Fat 10.4 g
- Saturated Fat 1.4 g
- Cholesterol 0 mg
- Sodium 42 mg
- Total Carbs 17.1 g
- Fiber 4.2 g Sugar 8.2 g
- Protein 12 g

CHAPTER 12:

Dessert Recipes

170. Ketogenic Lava Cake

Preparation time: 10 minutes
Cooking time: 10 minutes
Servings: 2 Servings
Ingredients:

- 2 Oz of dark chocolate; you should at least use chocolate of 85% cocoa solids
- 1 Tablespoon super-fine almond flour
- 2 Oz of unsalted almond butter
- 2 Large eggs

Directions:
1. Heat your oven to a temperature of about 350 Fahrenheit.
2. Grease 2 heat-proof ramekins with almond butter.
3. Now, melt the chocolate and the almond butter and stir very well.
4. Beat the eggs very well with a mixer.
5. Add the eggs to the chocolate and the butter mixture and mix very well with almond flour and the swerve; then stir.
6. Pour the dough into 2 ramekins.
7. Bake for about 9 to 10 minutes.
8. Turn the cakes over plates and serve with pomegranate seeds!

Nutrition:

- Calories: 459
- Fat: 39 g
- Carbohydrates: 3.5 g
- Fiber: 0.8 g
- Protein: 11.7 g

171. Keto Donuts

Preparation time: 5 minutes
Cooking time: 0 minutes
Servings: 4 Servings
Ingredients:
For the donut ingredients:

- 1/2 Cup sifted almond flour
- 3 to 4 tablespoons coconut milk
- 2 Large eggs
- 2 to 3 tablespoons granulated stevia
- 1 Teaspoon Keto-friendly baking powder
- 1 Heap teaspoon apple cider vinegar
- 1 Pinch salt
- 1 and 1/2 Tablespoon sifted cacao powder
- 3 Teaspoons Ceylon cinnamon
- 1 Teaspoon powdered vanilla bean
- 1 Tablespoon grass-fed ghee
- 2 Tablespoons Coconut oil for greasing

For the Icing ingredients:

- 4 Tablespoons of melted coconut butter with 1 to 2 teaspoons of coconut oil

Optional garnishing ingredients:

- Edible rose petals, or shredded cacao

Directions:
1. Preheat the oven to a temperature of about 350 degrees.
2. Grease a donut tray with the coconut oil.
3. Stir all together the sifted almond flour with the coconut milk, eggs, the granulated stevia, the Keto-friendly baking powder, the apple cider vinegar, the salt, the sifted cocoa powder, the Ceylon cinnamon, the powdered vanilla bean and the grass-fed ghee.
4. Mix your donut ingredients until they are evenly combined.
5. Divide the obtained batter into the donut moulds making sure to fill each to 3/4 full.
6. Bake for about 8 minutes; then remove the tray from the oven and carefully transfer it to a wire rack.
7. Serve and enjoy your donut or top it with the icing and the garnish of your choice.
8. Serve and enjoy your delicious treat!

Nutrition:

- Calories: 122
- Fat: 6.8 g
- Carbohydrates: 13.5 g
- Fiber: 2.3 g
- Protein: 3 g

172. Coconut Milk Pear Shake

Preparation time: 2 minutes
Cooking time: 0 minutes
Servings: 3-4 Servings
Ingredients:

- 4 Ripe chopped pears
- 4 lettuce leaves finely torn into pieces
- 1/4 Cup unsweetened coconut milk
- 5 Dried and toasted Almonds
- 4 Leaves mint
- 2 Tablespoons unsweetened orange juice
- 1/2 Tablespoon apple sauce
- 5 ice cubes

Directions:
1. Place the chopped pears in the blender.
2. Add the lettuce leaves.
3. Pour in the almond milk and the rest of the ingredients with the ice cubes.
4. Blend all of your ingredients for around 3 minutes.
5. Serve and enjoy!

Nutrition:
- Calories: 60
- Fat: 3 g
- Carbohydrates: 2.8 g
- Fiber: 1 g
- Protein: 3 g

173.   Cocoa Mousse

Preparation time: 3 minutes
Cooking time: 0 minutes
Servings: 2 Servings
Ingredients:
- 1 Cup Heavy Whipping coconut Cream
- 1/4 Cup sifted, unsweetened cocoa powder
- 1/4 Cup Swerve
- 1 Teaspoon Vanilla extract
- 1/4 Teaspoon kosher salt

Directions:
1. Start by whisking the cream until it starts stiffening.
2. Add in the stevia, the vanilla and the salt, and whisk your ingredients very well.
3. Add the cocoa powder to your ingredients and whisk again.
4. Serve and enjoy your Cocoa mousse!

Nutrition:
- Calories: 218
- Fat: 23 g
- Carbohydrates: 5 g
- Fiber: 1 g
- Protein: 3 g

174.   Coconut Ice Cream

Preparation time: 3 minutes
Cooking time: 0 minutes
Servings: 2 Servings
Ingredients:
- 2 Cups canned coconut milk
- 1/3 Cup stevia
- 1/8 Teaspoon salt
- 1 1/2 tsp pure vanilla extract or vanilla bean paste

Directions:
1. Make sure to use full-fat canned coconut milk.
2. You can also use the seeds of a vanilla bean instead of the extract.
3. Now, to make the ice cream, mix the milk with the Swerve the salt and the vanilla extract.
4. If you own an ice cream machine, you can simply churn by following the manufacturer's instructions.
5. Freeze the obtained mixture into ice cube trays, then blend in a blender on a high-speed; you can use a Vitamix, for example.
6. Freeze the ice cream for about 30 minutes.
7. Serve and enjoy your ice cream!

Nutrition:
- Calories: 283
- Fat: 21.5 g
- Carbohydrates: 5.1 g
- Fiber: 1.3 g
- Protein: 3.2 g

175.   Fruit Pizza

Preparation time: 5 minutes
Cooking time: 10 minutes
Servings: 4
Ingredients:
- 1 teaspoon maple syrup
- 1/4 teaspoon vanilla extract
- 1/2 cup coconut milk yogurt
- 2 round slices watermelon
- 1/2 cup blackberries, sliced
- 1/2 cup strawberries, sliced
- 2 tablespoons coconut flakes (unsweetened)

Directions:
1. Mix maple syrup, vanilla and yogurt in a bowl.
2. Spread the mixture on top of the watermelon slice.
3. Top with the berries and coconut flakes.

Nutrition:
- Calories 70;
- Carbohydrate 14.6 g
- Protein 1.2 g

176. Choco Peppermint Cake

Preparation time: 5 minutes
Cooking time: 10 minutes
Servings: 4
Ingredients:
- Cooking spray
- 1/3 cup oil
- 15 oz. package chocolate cake mix
- 3 eggs, beaten
- 1 cup water
- 1/4 teaspoon peppermint extract

Directions:
1. Spray slow cooker with oil.
2. Mix all the ingredients in a bowl.
3. Use an electric mixer on medium speed setting to mix ingredients for 2 minutes.
4. Pour the mixture into the slow cooker.
5. Cover the pot and cook on low for 3 hours.
6. Let cool before slicing and serving.

Nutrition:
- Calories 185; Carbohydrate 27 g
- Protein 3.8 g

177. Roasted Mango

Preparation time: 5 minutes
Cooking time: 10 minutes
Servings: 4
Ingredients:
- 2 mangoes, sliced
- 2 teaspoons crystallized ginger, chopped
- 2 teaspoons orange zest
- 2 tablespoons coconut flakes (unsweetened)

Directions:
1. Preheat your oven to 350 degrees F.
2. Add mango slices in custard cups.
3. Top with the ginger, orange zest and coconut flakes.
4. Bake in the oven for 10 minutes.

Nutrition:
- Calories 89; Carbohydrate 20 g
- Protein 0.8 g

178. Roasted Plums

Preparation time: 5 minutes
Cooking time: 10 minutes
Servings: 4
Ingredients:
- Cooking spray
- 6 plums, sliced
- 1/2 cup pineapple juice (unsweetened)
- 1 tablespoon brown sugar
- 2 tablespoons brown sugar
- 1/4 teaspoon ground cardamom
- 1/2 teaspoon ground cinnamon
- 1/8 teaspoon ground cumin

Directions:
1. Combine all the ingredients in a baking pan.
2. Roast in the oven at 450 degrees F for 20 minutes.

Nutrition:
- Calories 102;
- Carbohydrate 18.7 g
- Protein 2 g

179. Figs with Honey & Yogurt

Preparation time: 5 minutes
Cooking time: 10 minutes
Servings: 4
Ingredients:
- 1/2 teaspoon vanilla
- 8 oz. nonfat yogurt
- 2 figs, sliced
- 1 tablespoon walnuts, chopped and toasted
- 2 teaspoons honey

Directions:
1. Stir vanilla into yogurt.
2. Mix well.
3. Top with the figs and sprinkle with walnuts.
4. Drizzle with honey and serve.

Nutrition:
- Calories 157; Carbohydrate 24 g
- Protein 7 g

180. Flourless Chocolate Cake

Preparation time: 10 minutes
Cooking time: 45 minutes
Servings: 6
Ingredients:
- 1/2 Cup stevia
- 12 Ounces unsweetened baking chocolate
- 2/3 Cup ghee
- 1/3 Cup warm water
- 1/4 Teaspoon salt
- 4 Large pastured eggs
- 2 Cups boiling water

Directions:
1. Line the bottom of a 9-inch pan of a spring form with parchment paper.
2. Heat the water in a small pot; then add the salt and the stevia over the water until wait until the mixture becomes completely dissolved.
3. Melt the baking chocolate into a double boiler or simply microwave it for about 30 seconds.
4. Mix the melted chocolate and the butter in a large bowl with an electric mixer.
5. Beat in your hot mixture; then crack in the egg and whisk after adding each of the eggs.
6. Pour the obtained mixture into your prepared spring form tray.
7. Wrap the spring form tray with foil paper.
8. Place the spring form tray in a large cake tray and add boiling water right to the outside; make sure the depth doesn't exceed 1 inch.
9. Bake the cake into the water bath for about 45 minutes at a temperature of about 350 F.
10. Remove the tray from the boiling water and transfer it to a wire to cool.
11. Let the cake chill overnight in the refrigerator.

Nutrition:
- Calories 295;
- Carbohydrates 6 g
- Fiber 4 g

181. Waffles

Preparation time: 20 minutes
Cooking time: 30 minutes
Servings: 3
Ingredients:
For Ketogenic waffles:
- 8 Oz cream cheese
- 5 Large pastured eggs
- 1/3 Cup coconut flour
- 1/2 Teaspoon Xanthan gum
- 1 Pinch salt
- 1/2 Teaspoon vanilla extract
- 2 Tablespoons Swerve
- 1/4 Teaspoon baking soda
- 1/3 Cup almond milk

Optional Ingredients:
- 1/2 Teaspoon cinnamon pie spice
- 1/4 Teaspoon almond extract

For low-carb Maple Syrup:
- 1 Cup of water
- 1 Tablespoon Maple flavor
- 3/4 Cup powdered Swerve
- 1 Tablespoon almond butter
- 1/2 Teaspoon Xanthan gum

Directions:
For the waffles:
1. Make sure all your ingredients are exactly at room temperature.
2. Place all your ingredients for the waffles from cream cheese to pastured eggs, coconut flour, Xanthan gum, salt, vanilla extract, the Swerve, the baking soda and the almond milk except for the almond milk with the help of a processor.
3. Blend your ingredients until it becomes smooth and creamy; then transfer the batter to a bowl.
4. Add the almond milk and mix your ingredients with a spatula.
5. Heat a waffle maker to a temperature of high.
6. Spray your waffle maker with coconut oil and add about 1/4 of the batter in it evenly with a spatula into your waffle iron.
7. Close your waffle and cook until you get the color you want.
8. Carefully remove the waffles to a platter.

For the Ketogenic Maple Syrup:
1. Place 1 and 1/4 cups of water, the swerve and the maple in a small pan and bring to a boil over low heat; then let simmer for about 10 minutes.
2. Add the coconut oil.
3. Sprinkle the Xanthan gum over the top of the waffle and use an immersion blender to blend smoothly.
4. Serve and enjoy your delicious waffles!

Nutrition:
- Calories 316;
- Carbohydrates 7 g
- Fiber 3 g

182. Pumpkin & Banana Ice Cream

Preparation time: 5 minutes
Cooking time: 10 minutes
Servings: 4
Ingredients:
- 15 oz. pumpkin puree
- 4 bananas, sliced and frozen

- 1 teaspoon pumpkin pie spice
- Chopped pecans

Directions:
1. Add pumpkin puree, bananas and pumpkin pie spice in a food processor.
2. Pulse until smooth.
3. Chill in the refrigerator.
4. Garnish with pecans.

Nutrition:
- Calories 71;
- Carbohydrate 18 g
- Protein 1.2 g

183. Brulee Oranges

Preparation time: 5 minutes
Cooking time: 10 minutes
Servings: 4
Ingredients:
- 4 oranges, sliced into segments
- 1 teaspoon ground cardamom
- 6 teaspoons brown sugar
- 1 cup nonfat Greek yogurt

Directions:
1. Preheat your broiler.
2. Arrange orange slices in a baking pan.
3. In a bowl, mix the cardamom and sugar.
4. Sprinkle mixture on top of the oranges. Broil for 5 minutes.
5. Serve oranges with yogurt.

Nutrition:
- Calories 168;
- Carbohydrate 26.9 g
- Protein 6.8 g

184. Frozen Lemon & Blueberry

Preparation time: 5 minutes
Cooking time: 10 minutes
Servings: 4
Ingredients:
- 6 cup fresh blueberries
- 8 sprigs fresh thyme
- 3/4 cup light brown sugar
- 1 teaspoon lemon zest
- 1/4 cup lemon juice
- 2 cups water

Directions:
1. Add blueberries, thyme and sugar in a pan over medium heat.
2. Cook for 6 to 8 minutes.
3. Transfer mixture to a blender.
4. Remove thyme sprigs.
5. Stir in the remaining ingredients.
6. Pulse until smooth.
7. Strain mixture and freeze for 1 hour.

Nutrition:
- Calories 78;
- Carbohydrate 20 g
- Protein 3 g

185. Peanut Butter Choco Chip Cookies

Preparation time: 5 minutes
Cooking time: 10 minutes
Servings: 4
Ingredients:
- 1 egg
- 1/2 cup light brown sugar
- 1 cup natural unsweetened peanut butter
- Pinch salt
- 1/4 cup dark chocolate chips

Directions:
1. Preheat your oven to 375° F.
2. Mix egg sugar, peanut butter, salt and chocolate chips in a bowl.
3. Form into cookies and place in a baking pan.
4. Bake the cookie for 10 minutes.
5. Let cool before serving.

Nutrition:
- Calories 159;
- Carbohydrate 12 g
- Protein 4.3 g

186. Watermelon Sherbet

Preparation time: 5 minutes
Cooking time: 3 minutes
Servings: 4
Ingredients:
- 6 cups watermelon, sliced into cubes
- 14 oz. almond milk
- 1 tablespoon honey
- 1/4 cup lime juice
- Salt to taste

Directions:
1. Freeze watermelon for 4 hours.
2. Add frozen watermelon and other ingredients in a blender.

3. Blend until smooth.
4. Transfer to a container with seal.
5. Seal and freeze for 4 hours.

Nutrition:
- Calories 132; Carbohydrate 24.5 g
- Protein 3.1 g

187. Strawberry & Mango Ice Cream

Preparation time: 5 minutes
Cooking time: 10 minutes
Servings: 4
Ingredients:
- 8 oz. strawberries, sliced
- 12 oz. mango, sliced into cubes
- 1 tablespoon lime juice

Directions:
1. Add all ingredients in a food processor.
2. Pulse for 2 minutes.
3. Chill before serving.

Nutrition:
- Calories 70; Carbohydrate 17.4 g
- Protein 1.1 g

188. Ice Cream Brownie Cake

Preparation time: 5 minutes
Cooking time: 10 minutes
Servings: 4
Ingredients:
- Cooking spray
- 12 oz. no-sugar brownie mix
- 1/4 cup oil
- 2 egg whites
- 3 tablespoons water
- 2 cups sugar-free ice cream

Directions:
1. Preheat your oven to 325° F.
2. Spray your baking pan with oil.
3. Mix brownie mix, oil, egg whites and water in a bowl.
4. Pour into the baking pan.
5. Bake for 25 minutes.
6. Let cool.
7. Freeze brownie for 2 hours.
8. Spread ice cream over the brownie.
9. Freeze for 8 hours.

Nutrition:
- Calories 198; Carbohydrate 33 g
- Protein 3 g

189. Air Fried Sugar-Free Chocolate Soufflé

Preparation Time: 15 minutes
Cooking Time: 15 minutes
Servings: 2
Ingredients:
- 1/3 cup Milk
- 2 tbsp. Butter soft to melted
- 1 tbsp. Flour
- 2 tbsp. Splenda
- 1 Egg Yolk
- 1/4 cup Sugar-Free Chocolate Chips
- 2 egg whites
- ½ teaspoon cream of tartar
- ½ teaspoon Vanilla Extract

Directions:
1. Grease the ramekins with spray oil or softened butter.
2. Sprinkle with any sugar alternative, make sure to cover them.
3. Let the air fryer preheat to 325°-330° F
4. Melt the chocolate in a microwave-safe bowl. Mix every 30 seconds until fully melted.
5. Or use a double boiler method.
6. Melt the one and a half tablespoons of butter over low-medium heat. In a small-sized skillet.
7. Once the butter has melted, then whisk in the flour. Keep whisking until thickened. Then turn the heat off.
8. Add the egg whites with cream of tartar, with the whisk attachment, in a stand mixer, mix until peaks forms.
9. Meanwhile, combine the ingredients in a melted chocolate bowl, add the flour mixture and melted butter to chocolate, and blend. Add in the vanilla extract, egg yolks, remaining sugar alternative.
10. Fold the egg white peaks gently with the ingredients into the bowl.
11. Add the mix into ramekins about 3/4 full of five-ounce ramekins
12. Let it bake for 12-14 minutes, or until done.

Nutrition:
- Calories: 288 Carbohydrates: 5 g
- Protein: 6 g
- Fat: 24 g

190. Easy Air Fryer Brownies

Preparation Time: 10 minutes
Cooking Time: 10 minutes
Servings: 2
Ingredients:
- 2 tbsp. of Baking Chips
- 1/3 cup of Almond Flour
- 1 Egg
- ½ teaspoon of Baking Powder
- 3 tbsp. of Powdered Sweetener (sugar alternative)
- 2 tbsp. of Cocoa Powder (Unsweetened)
- 2 tbsp. of chopped Pecans
- 4 tbsp. of melted Butter

Directions:
1. Let the air fryer preheat to 350° F
2. In a large bowl, add cocoa powder, almond flour, Swerve sugar substitute, and baking powder, give it a good mix.
3. Add melted butter and crack in the egg in the dry ingredients.
4. Mix well until combined and smooth.
5. Fold in the chopped pecans and baking chips.
6. Take two ramekins to grease them well with softened butter. Add the batter to them.
7. Bake for ten minutes. Make sure to place them as far from the heat source from the top in the air fryer.
8. Take the brownies out from the air fryer and let them cool for five minutes.
9. Serve with your favorite toppings and enjoy.

Nutrition:
- Calories: 201
- Fat 10.2 g
- Protein: 8.7 g
- Carbs: 14.1 g

191. Air Fryer Apple Fritter

Preparation Time: 10 minutes
Cooking Time: 10 minutes
Servings: 3
Ingredients:
- ½ apple (Pink Lady Apple or Honey crisp) peeled, finely chopped
- ½ cup All-Purpose Flour
- 1 teaspoon Baking Powder
- ¼ teaspoon Kosher Salt
- ½ teaspoon Ground Cinnamon
- 2 Tbsp. Brown Sugar or sugar alternative
- 1/8 teaspoon Ground Nutmeg
- 3 Tbsp. Greek Yogurt (Fat-Free)
- 1 tablespoon of Butter

For the glaze:
- 2 Tbsp. Powdered Sugar
- ½ tablespoon Water

Directions:
1. In a big mixing bowl, add baking powder, nutmeg brown sugar (or alternative), flour, cinnamon, and salt. Mix it well,
2. With the help of a fork or cutter, slice the butter until crumbly. It should look like wet sand.
3. Add the chopped apple and coat well, then add fat-free Greek yogurt.
4. keep stirring or tossing until everything together, and a crumbly dough forms
5. Put the dough on a clean surface and with your hands, knead it into a ball form.
6. Flatten the dough in an oval shape about a half-inch thick. It is okay, even if it's not the perfect size or shape.
7. Spray the basket of the air fryer with cooking spray generously. Put the dough in the air fry for 12-14 minutes at 375°F cook until light golden brown.
8. For making the glaze mix, the ingredients, and with the help of a brush, pour over the apple fritter when it comes out from the air fryer.
9. Slice and serve after cooling for 5 minutes.

Nutrition:
- Calories: 200
- Fat: 12 g
- Protein: 9.8 g
- Carbs: 14 g

192. Grain-free Molten Lava Cakes (Air Fryer)

Preparation Time: 5 minutes
Cooking Time: 10 minutes
Servings: 2
Ingredients:
- 2 large eggs
- ½ cup of chocolate chips, you can use dark chocolate
- 2 tbsp. coconut flour

- 2 tablespoons of honey as a sugar substitute
- A dash of sea salt
- ½ teaspoon of baking soda
- Butter and cocoa powder for (two small ramekins)
- 1/4 cup butter or grass-fed butter

Directions:
1. Let the air fryer preheat to 370°F.
2. Grease the ramekins with soft butter and sprinkle with cocoa powder. It will stick to the butter. Turn the ramekins upside down, so excess cocoa powder will fall out. Set it aside.
3. In a double boiler or microwave, safe bowl, melt the butter and chocolate chips together, stir every 15 seconds. Make sure to mix well to combine.
4. In a large bowl, crack the eggs and whisk with either honey or sugar, mix well. Add in the baking soda, sea salt, and coconut flour. Gently fold everything.
5. Then add the melted chocolate chip and butter mixture to the egg flour, and honey mixture. Mix well, so everything combines.
6. Pour the batter in those two prepared ramekins.
7. Let them air fry for ten minutes. Then take them out from the air fryer and let it cool for 3 or 4 minutes.
8. When cool enough to handle, run a knife along the edges so the cake will out easier.
9. After flipping them upside down on a serving plate.
10. Top with mint leaves and coconut cream, raspberries, if you want. Serve right away and enjoy.

Nutrition:
- Calories: 217
- Fat: 12 g
- Protein: 9.9 g
- Carbs: 14 g

193. Lemon Custard

Preparation time: 10 minutes
Cooking time: 3 hours
Servings: 4
Ingredients:
- 2 cups whipping cream or coconut cream
- 5 egg yolks
- 1 tablespoon lemon zest
- 1 teaspoon vanilla extract
- 1/4 cup fresh lemon juice, squeezed
- 1/2 teaspoon liquid stevia
- Lightly sweetened whipped cream

Directions:
1. Whisk egg yolks together with lemon zest, liquid stevia, lemon zest and vanilla in a bowl, and then whisk in heavy cream.
2. Divide the mixture among 4 small jars or ramekins.
3. To the bottom of a slow cooker, add a rack, and then add ramekins on top of the rack and add enough water to cover half of the ramekins.
4. Close the lid and cook for 3 hours on low. Remove ramekins.
5. Let cool to room temperature, and then place into the refrigerator to cool completely for about 3 hours.
6. When through, top with the whipped cream and serve. Enjoy!

Nutrition:
- Calories: 319; Fat: 30 g
- Total carbs: 3 g Protein: 7 g

194. Slow Cooker Peaches

Preparation time: 10 minutes
Cooking time: 4 hours 20 minutes
Servings: 4-6
Ingredients:
- 4 cups peaches, sliced
- 2/3 cup rolled oats
- 1/3 cup Bisques
- 1/4 teaspoon cinnamon
- 1/2 cup brown sugar
- 1/2 cup granulated sugar

Directions:
1. Spray the slow cooker pot with a cooking spray.
2. Mix oats, Bisques, cinnamon and all the sugars in the pot.
3. Add peaches and stir well to combine. Cook on low for 4-6 hours.

Nutrition:
- Calories: 617; Fat: 3.6 g
- Total carbs: 13 g
- Protein: 9 g

195. Tiramisu Shots

Preparation time: 5 minutes
Cooking time: 10 minutes
Servings: 4
Ingredients:
- 1 pack silken tofu
- 1 oz. dark chocolate, finely chopped
- 1/4 cup sugar substitute
- 1 teaspoon lemon juice
- 1/4 cup brewed espresso
- Pinch salt
- 24 slices angel food cake
- Cocoa powder (unsweetened)

Directions:
1. Add tofu, chocolate, sugar substitute, lemon juice, espresso and salt in a food processor.
2. Pulse until smooth.
3. Add angel food cake pieces into shot glasses.
4. Drizzle with the cocoa powder.
5. Pour the tofu mixture on top.
6. Top with the remaining angel food cake pieces.
7. Chill for 30 minutes and serve.

Nutrition:
- Calories: 75;
- Carbohydrate: 12 g
- Protein: 2.9 g

196. Keto Vanilla Mug Cake

Preparation time: 5 Minutes
Cooking time: 1 Minute
Servings: 1
Ingredients:
- 1/4 tsp. Baking Powder
- 1 tbsp. Butter, melted
- 1 tsp. Vanilla Extract
- 2 tbsp. Cream Cheese
- 1 Egg
- 2 tbsp. Coconut Flour
- 6 Raspberries, frozen
- 1 tbsp. Low-Carb Sweetener, granulated

Directions:
1. Place butter and cream cheese in a large mug and heat on high power for 20 seconds.
2. Spoon in coconut flour, baking powder, sweetener, and vanilla to it. Combine.
3. Add the egg to it and stir it again.
4. Scrape down the sides and press the six raspberries to it.
5. Heat the batter again for 1 minute and 20 seconds on high power.
6. Allow it to cool and set aside.

Nutrition:
- Calories: 342
- Carbohydrates: 4.5 g
- Proteins: 9 g
- Fat: 27 g
- Sodium: 17 mg

197. Chia Pudding

Preparation time: 10 Minutes
Cooking time: 0 Minutes
Servings: 1
Ingredients:
- 2 tbsp. Chia Seeds
- 1 cup Almond Milk
- 1 tsp. Stevia, vanilla flavored

Directions:
1. Mix the chia seeds and almond milk thoroughly until combined well.
2. Set it aside for overnight in the refrigerator.
3. Serve and enjoy. You can top with topping of your choice like berries, nuts, etc.

Nutrition:
- Calories: 151
- Carbohydrates: 1.5 g
- Proteins: 5 g
- Fat: 10 g
- Sodium: 328 mg

198. Chocolate Mousse

Preparation time: 10 Minutes
Cooking time: 5 Minutes
Servings: 4
Ingredients:
- 1/4 cup Cocoa Powder, unsweetened
- 1 cup Heavy Whipping Cream
- 1 tsp. Vanilla Extract
- 1/4 cup Low-Carb Sweetener, powdered
- 1/4 tsp. Salt

Directions:
1. Place the whipping cream in a large mixing bowl and whisk it with a mixer until you get stiff peaks.

2. Stir in the remaining ingredients and whisk until everything comes together.
3. Serve and enjoy.

Nutrition:
- Calories: 218
- Carbohydrates: 3 g
- Proteins: 2 g
- Fat: 23 g
- Sodium: 29 mg

199. Chocolate Ice Cream

Preparation time: 10 Minutes
Cooking time: 0 + 2 Hours Setting Time
Servings: 1 to 2

Ingredients:
- 1/2 cup Almond Milk, unsweetened
- 2 1/2 oz. Greek Yoghurt, fat-free
- 2 tbsp. Stevia
- 1/2 oz. Protein Powder
- 1 tsp. Vanilla Extract
- 1 tsp. Cocoa Powder, unsweetened

Directions:
1. Place yogurt, almond milk, cocoa powder, stevia, and protein powder in a high-speed blender.
2. Blend them for few minutes or until you get a smooth mixture.
3. Place in the freezer to set.
4. Take out the ice cream every 30 seconds and blend. Repeat the procedure for about 2 hours until you get the right consistency without any ice blocks.
5. Serve and enjoy.

Nutrition:
- Calories: 127
- Carbohydrates: 5.6 g
- Proteins: 20.1 g
- Fat: 2.2 g
- Sodium: 150 mg

CHAPTER 13:

Other Recipes

200. Italian Eggplant Stew

Preparation time: 10 minutes
Cooking time: 15 minutes
Servings: 4
Ingredients:
- 1 red onion, chopped
- 2 garlic cloves, chopped
- 1 bunch parsley, chopped
- Salt and black pepper to the taste
- 1 teaspoon oregano, dried
- 2 eggplants, cut into medium chunks
- 2 tablespoons olive oil
- 2 tablespoons capers, chopped
- 1 handful green olives, pitted and sliced
- 5 tomatoes, chopped
- 3 tablespoons herb vinegar

Directions:
1. Heat up a pan that fits your air fryer with the oil over medium heat, add eggplant, oregano, salt and pepper, stir and cook for 5 minutes.
2. Add garlic, onion, parsley, capers, olives, vinegar and tomatoes, stir, introduce in your air fryer and cook at 360 degrees F for 15 minutes.
3. Divide into bowls and serve.

Nutrition:
- Calories 170,
- Fat 13 g
- Fiber 3 g
- Carbs 5 g
- Protein 7 g

201. Indian Potatoes

Preparation time: 10 minutes
Cooking time: 12 minutes
Servings: 4
Ingredients:
- 1 tablespoon coriander seeds
- 1 tablespoon cumin seeds
- Salt and black pepper to the taste
- 1/2 teaspoon turmeric powder
- 1/2 teaspoon red chili powder
- 1 teaspoon pomegranate powder
- 1 tablespoon pickled mango, chopped
- 2 teaspoons fenugreek, dried
- 5 potatoes, boiled, peeled and cubed
- 2 tablespoons olive oil

Directions:
1. Heat up a pan that fits your air fryer with the oil over medium heat, add coriander and cumin seeds, stir and cook for 2 minutes.
2. Add salt, pepper, turmeric, chili powder, pomegranate powder, mango, fenugreek and potatoes, toss, introduce in your air fryer and cook at 360° F for 10 minutes.
3. Divide among plates and serve hot.

Nutrition:
- Calories 251,
- Fat 7 g
- Fiber 4 g
- Carbs 12 g
- Protein 7 g

202. Broccoli and Tomatoes Air Fried Stew

Preparation time: 10 minutes
Cooking time: 20 minutes
Servings: 4
Ingredients:
- 1 broccoli head, florets separated
- 2 teaspoons coriander seeds
- 1 tablespoon olive oil
- 1 yellow onion, chopped
- Salt and black pepper to the taste
- A pinch of red pepper, crushed
- 1 small ginger piece, chopped
- 1 garlic clove, minced
- 28 ounces canned tomatoes, pureed

Directions:
1. Heat up a pan that fits your air fryer with the oil over medium heat, add onions, salt, pepper and red pepper, stir and cook for 7 minutes.
2. Add ginger, garlic, coriander seeds, tomatoes and broccoli, stir, introduce in your air fryer and cook at 360 degrees F for 12 minutes.
3. Divide into bowls and serve.

Nutrition:
- Calories 150,
- Fat 4 g
- Fiber 2 g
- Carbs 7 g
- Protein 12 g

203. Collard Greens and Bacon

Preparation time: 10 minutes
Cooking time: 12 minutes
Servings: 4
Ingredients:
- 1 pound collard greens
- 3 bacon strips, chopped
- 1/4 cup cherry tomatoes, halved
- 1 tablespoon apple cider vinegar
- 2 tablespoons chicken stock
- Salt and black pepper to the taste

Directions:
1. Heat up a pan that fits your air fryer over medium heat, add bacon, stir and cook 1-2 minutes
2. Add tomatoes, collard greens, vinegar, stock, salt and pepper, stir, introduce in your air fryer and cook at 320 degrees F for 10 minutes.
3. Divide among plates and serve.

Nutrition:
- Calories 120,
- Fat 3 g
- Fiber 1 g
- Carbs 3 g
- Protein 7 g

204. Sesame Mustard Greens

Preparation time: 10 minutes
Cooking time: 11 minutes
Servings: 4
Ingredients:
- 2 garlic cloves, minced
- 1 pound mustard greens, torn
- 1 tablespoon olive oil
- 1/2 cup yellow onion, sliced
- Salt and black pepper to the taste
- 3 tablespoons veggie stock
- 1/4 teaspoon dark sesame oil

Directions:
1. Heat up a pan that fits your air fryer with the oil over medium heat, add onions, stir and brown them for 5 minutes.
2. Add garlic, stock, greens, salt and pepper, stir, introduce in your air fryer and cook at 350 degrees F for 6 minutes.
3. Add sesame oil, toss to coat, divide among plates and serve.

Nutrition:
- Calories 120,
- Fat 3 g
- Fiber 1 g
- Carbs 3 g
- Protein 7 g

205. Radish Hash

Preparation time: 10 minutes
Cooking time: 7 minutes
Servings: 4
Ingredients:
- 1/2 teaspoon onion powder
- 1 pound radishes, sliced
- 1/2 teaspoon garlic powder
- Salt and black pepper to the taste
- 4 eggs
- 1/3 cup parmesan, grated

Directions:
1. In a bowl, mix radishes with salt, pepper, onion and garlic powder, eggs and parmesan, and stir well.
2. Transfer radishes to a pan that fits your air fryer and cook at 350° F for 7 minutes.
3. Divide hash among plates and serve.

Nutrition:
- Calories 80,
- Fat 5 g
- Fiber 2 g
- Carbs 5 g
- Protein 7 g

206. Swiss Chard Salad

Preparation time: 10 minutes
Cooking time: 13 minutes
Servings: 4
Ingredients:
- 1 bunch Swiss chard, torn
- 2 tablespoons olive oil
- 1 small yellow onion, chopped
- A pinch of red pepper flakes
- 1/4 cup pine nuts, toasted
- 1/4 cup raisins
- 1 tablespoon balsamic vinegar
- Salt and black pepper to the taste

Directions:
1. Heat up a pan that fits your air fryer with the oil over medium heat, add chard and onions, stir and cook for 5 minutes.
2. Add salt, pepper, pepper flakes, raisins, pine nuts and vinegar, stir, introduce in your air fryer and cook at 350°F for 8 minutes.
3. Divide among plates and serve.

Nutrition:
- Calories 120,
- Fat 2 g
- Fiber 1 g
- Carbs 8 g
- Protein 8 g

207. Spanish Greens

Preparation time: 10 minutes
Cooking time: 8 minutes
Servings: 4
Ingredients:
- 1 apple, cored and chopped
- 1 yellow onion, sliced
- 3 tablespoons olive oil
- 1/4 cup raisins
- 6 garlic cloves, chopped
- 1/4 cup pine nuts, toasted
- 1/4 cup balsamic vinegar
- 5 cups mixed spinach and chard
- Salt and black pepper to the taste
- A pinch of nutmeg

Directions:
1. Heat up a pan that fits your air fryer with the oil over medium-high heat, add onion, stir and cook for 3 minutes.
2. Add apple, garlic, raisins, vinegar, mixed spinach and chard, nutmeg salt and pepper, stir, introduce in preheated air fryer and cook at 350 degrees F for 5 minutes.
3. Divide among plates, sprinkle pine nuts on top and serve.

Nutrition:
- Calories 120,
- Fat 1 g
- Fiber 2 g
- Carbs 3 g
- Protein 6 g

208. Rutabaga and Cherry Tomatoes Mix

Preparation time: 10 minutes
Cooking time: 15 minutes
Servings: 4
Ingredients:
- 1 tablespoon shallot, chopped
- 1 garlic clove, minced
- 3/4 cup cashews, soaked for a couple of hours and drained
- 2 tablespoons nutritional yeast
- 1/2 cup veggie stock
- Salt and black pepper to the taste
- 2 teaspoons lemon juice

For the pasta:
- 1 cup cherry tomatoes, halved
- 5 teaspoons olive oil
- 1/4 teaspoon garlic powder
- 2 rutabagas, peeled and cut into thick noodles

Directions:
1. Place tomatoes and rutabaga noodles into a pan that fits your air fryer, drizzle the oil over them, season with salt, black pepper and garlic powder, toss to coat and cook in your air fryer at 350 degrees F for 15 minutes.
2. Meanwhile, in a food processor, mix garlic with shallots, cashews, veggie stock, nutritional yeast, lemon juice, a pinch of sea salt and black pepper to the taste and blend well.
3. Divide rutabaga pasta on plates, top with tomatoes, drizzle the sauce over them and serve.

Nutrition:
- Calories 160,
- Fat 2 g
- Fiber 5 g
- Carbs 10 g
- Protein 8 g

209. Garlic Tomatoes

Preparation time: 10 minutes
Cooking time: 15 minutes
Servings: 4
Ingredients:
- 4 garlic cloves, crushed
- 1 pound mixed cherry tomatoes
- 3 thyme springs, chopped
- Salt and black pepper to the taste
- 1/4 cup olive oil

Directions:
1. In a bowl, mix tomatoes with salt, black pepper, garlic, olive oil and thyme, toss to coat, introduce in your air fryer and cook at 360 degrees F for 15 minutes.
2. Divide the tomato mix among plates and serve.

Nutrition:
- Calories 100,
- Fat 0 g
- Fiber 1 g
- Carbs 1 g
- Protein 6 g

Conclusion

Diabetes is a condition that can be exceptionally normal and can be risky. Diabetes is additionally a condition that can be managed. In case you are being treated for diabetes, it is huge that you take as much time as vital and that you are taking the best thought of yourself by accepting a reasonable eating plan, for instance, the Mediterranean eating routine or some other eating routine course of action that works for you. Ensure you eat sufficient food and exercise consistently to keep a sound weight. In case you're diabetic yet haven't began taking medication, see the specialist and check whether you're in danger for some other diabetes-related medical conditions.

Type 1 diabetes has the same warning symptoms as type 2 diabetes, but the signs and symptoms appear gradually over months or years, making it more difficult to spot and remember. Any of these signs and symptoms will appear even after the disease has advanced.

Each problem has hazard factors that, when present in an individual, favor infection movement. Diabetes is no special case. A portion of the danger factors for diabetes are recorded underneath.

Diabetes can strike someone at any age. Being too young or too old, on the other hand, means your body isn't in peak condition, which raises the risk of developing diabetes.

That sounds terrifying. Diabetes, on the other hand, is only caused by a combination of these risk factors. The majority of risk factors can be reduced by taking steps. Create a healthier lifestyle, take care of your habits, and try to lower your blood glucose sugar by limiting your sugar intake, for example. If you notice you're becoming prediabetic or overweight, for example, there's always something you can do to improve your condition. Recent research suggests that improving healthy eating habits and low-carbohydrate diets, as well as losing weight and living an active lifestyle, may help protect you from developing diabetes, especially type 2 diabetes, by reducing the risk factors associated with the disease.

You may also do an oral glucose tolerance test, which involves a fasting glucose test followed by a sugary drink and a 2 hour blood glucose test to see how the body reacts to glucose meals. Because of the action of insulin, blood glucose levels could drop 2 hours after a sugary meal in healthy people.

Since they have no other choice, people with type 1 diabetes should put forth insulin attempts to manage their diabetes. People with type 2 diabetes can deal with their diabetes with a sensible eating routine and step by step genuine work, anyway they should bring glucose-cutting down drugs, which can be taken as tablets or as implantations.

All of the above points to the conclusion that a starchy diet should be avoided due to its ability to increase blood glucose levels. Too much carbohydrates may cause insulin resistance and pancreatic exhaustion, as well as weight gain and the risk factors for cardiovascular disease and hypertension that come with it. The alternative is to reduce your sugar consumption, which will reduce the body's need for insulin while also increasing fat burning.

Index of Recipes

A

Air Fried Sugar-Free Chocolate Soufflé	106
Air Fryer Apple Fritter	107
Apple Topped French Toast	25
Asian Noodle Salad	81
Asparagus and Scallop Skillet With Lemony	36
Asparagus with Scallops	35
Authentic Gazpacho	87
Autumn Pork Chops with Red Cabbage and Apples	56
Avocado and Tempeh Bacon Wraps	98

B

Bacon & Chicken Patties	56
Barbecue Beef Brisket	50
Basil-Parmesan Crusted Salmon	64
Beef & Asparagus	49
Beef Barley Soup	91
Beef Chili	51
Beef Steaks with Green Asparagus	55
Blackened Tilapia with Mango Salsa	41
Blueberry and Chicken Salad	83
Blueberry Breakfast Cake	28
Breaded Cod	61
Broccoli and Chicken Soup	92
Broccoli and Tomatoes Air Fried Stew	113
Broiled Cod Fillets with Garlic Mango Salsa	66
Brulee Oranges	105
Buckwheat Grouts Breakfast Bowl	29
Buffalo Bites	98
Buffalo Chicken Salads	83
Butter Cod with Asparagus	35
Butter Cod with Lemony Asparagus	67
Buttered Salmon	63
Butter-Lemon Grilled Cod on Asparagus	36

C

Cabbage Slaw Salad	81
Cafe Mocha Smoothies	25
Cajun Catfish	38
Carrot Hummus	75
Cauliflower Breakfast Hash	25
Cheese Crisp Crackers	96
Cheese Spinach Waffles	25
Cheeseburger Soup	90
Chia Pudding	109
Chili Sin Carne	75
Chipotle Chili Pork Chops	44
Choco Peppermint Cake	103
Chocolate Ice Cream	110
Chocolate Mousse	109
Cilantro Lime Shrimp	37
Cinnamon Apple Chips	99
Cinnamon Apple Granola	26
Cobb Salad	79
Cocoa Mousse	102
Coconut Breakfast Porridge	26
Coconut Ice Cream	102
Coconut Milk Pear Shake	101
Cod Fillet Quinoa Asparagus Bowl	67
Coffee-and-Herb-Marinated Steak	46
Coffee-Steamed Carrots	71
Collard Greens and Bacon	114
Cottage Cheese Pancakes	27
Creamy Chicken Soup	92
Creamy Cod Fillet with Quinoa and Asparagus	35
Creole Braised Sirloin	56
Crispy Baked Cheese Puffs	95
Crispy Chicken Wings	57
Crispy Fish Sticks in Air Fryer	63
Cucumber and Kidney Bean Salad	78

D

Delicious Lamb Chops	58

E

Easy Air Fryer Brownies	107
Eggplant Curry	74

F

Figs with Honey & Yogurt	103
Flourless Chocolate Cake	103
Fried Tofu Hotpot	75
Frozen Lemon & Blueberry	105
Fruit Pizza	102
Fruity Cod with Salsa	66

G

Garlic Chicken Balls	55
Garlic Sautéed Spinach	75
Garlic Tomatoes	116
Ginger Cod Chard Bake	65
Ginger-Garlic Cod Cooked in Paper	40

Ginger-Glazed Salmon and Broccoli 39
Grain, Seafood, and Fruit Salad 80
Grain-free Molten Lava Cakes (Air Fryer) 107
Green Salad with Blackberries Vinaigrette 77
Guinness Beef Stew with Cauliflower Mash 93

H

Halibut Ceviche with Cilantro 64
Ham & Jicama Hash 27
Herb Butter Lamb Chops 57
Herb Garlic Lamb Chops 58
Homestyle Herb Meatballs 44
Honey-Glazed Salmon 64
Hot & Spicy Mixed Nuts 97
Hot Maple Porridge 27

I

Ice Cream Brownie Cake 106
Indian Potatoes 113
Italian Beef 49
Italian Eggplant Stew 113
Italian Pork Chops 53

J

Jicama Hash Browns 28

K

Kale, Cantaloupe, and Chicken Salad 78
Keto Donuts 101
Keto Vanilla Mug Cake 109
Ketogenic Lava Cake 101
Kidney Bean Stew 74

L

Lamb with Broccoli & Carrots 50
Lemon Chili Salmon 60
Lemon Custard 108
Lemon Parsley White Fish Fillets 37
Lemony Dijon Meat Loaf 53
Lemony Salmon 62
Lentil and Chickpea Curry 74
Lentil and Eggplant Stew 74
Lentil Vegetable Soup 91
Lime Chicken Tortilla Soup 88
Lime-Parsley Lamb Cutlets 45
Lovely Porridge 32
Low Fat Roasties 72
Lower Carb Hummus 72

M

Mashed Pumpkin 71
Mediterranean Steak Sandwiches 45
Moroccan Eggplant Stew 89
Mortadella & Bacon Balls 95
Mozzarella Sticks 97
Mu Shu Lunch Pork 55
Mushroom, Zucchini, and Onion Frittata 30

O

Oatmeal Butterscotch Cookies 96
Orange-Marinated Pork Tenderloin 44

P

Parmesan Cauliflower Mash 73
Parmesan-Topped Acorn Squash 72
Peach Muesli Bake 29
Peanut Butter Choco Chip Cookies 105
Peppercorn-Crusted Baked Salmon 38
Peppery Halibut Fillet with Beans 65
Plum & Pistachio Snack 98
Pork Chop Diane 43
Pork Chops with Grape Sauce 47
Pork Mushroom Stew 54
Pork Rolls 59
Pork Sausage Casserole 60
Pork Tenderloin with Bacon & Veggies 59
Pork Tenderloin with Bell Peppers 59
Pork with Cranberry Relish 47
Pumpkin & Banana Ice Cream 104
Pumpkin Spiced Almonds 96

Q

Quail Eggs & Prosciutto Wraps 96
Quick Clam Chowder 91

R

Radish Hash 114
Rainbow Black Bean Salad 82
Raspberry Almond Tart 95
Roasted Beef with Peppercorn Sauce 45
Roasted Halibut with Red Peppers, Green Beans, and Onions 41
Roasted Mango 103
Roasted Parsnips 72
Roasted Plums 103
Roasted Pork & Apples 47
Roasted Salmon with Honey-Mustard Sauce 39
Roasted Salmon with Salsa Verde 39
Rosemary Lemon Lamb Chops 58
Rosemary Potatoes 71
Rutabaga and Cherry Tomatoes Mix 115

S

Salmon Patties	61
Scallops and Asparagus Skillet	42
Sesame Mustard Greens	114
Sesame Pork with Mustard Sauce	48
Slow Cooker Peaches	108
Sofrito Steak and Veg Salad	79
Spanish Greens	115
Spiced Tilapia	63
Spicy Catfish	62
Spicy Jalapeno Popper Deviled Eggs	31
Spinach and Cheese Quiche	31
Spinach and Chicken Salad	78
Spinach, Pear, and Walnut Salad	80
Split Pea Soup with Carrots	89
Squash Medley	73
Steak with Mushroom Sauce	48
Steak with Tomato & Herbs	49
Steamed Asparagus	73
Steel-Cut Oatmeal Bowl with Fruit and Nuts	30
Strawberry & Mango Ice Cream	106
Summer Salad with Honey Dressing	77
Swiss Chard Salad	114

T

Taco Soup	90
Thai Shrimp Soup	88
Three Bean and Basil Salad	82
Tiramisu Shots	109
Tofu & Chia Seed Pudding	99
Tofu Curry	74
Tomato Kale Soup	87
Tomato Steak Kebabs	54
Tomato Tuna Melts	38
Tomato, Cucumber, and Avocado Salad	77
Tortilla Chips	97
Traditional Beef Stroganoff	46
Tropical Shrimp Cocktail	43
Tuna Burgers	61
Tuna Onion Broccoli Casserole	67

V

Vinegar Halibut	62

W

Waffles	104
Warm Barley and Squash Salad	82
Watermelon Sherbet	105
Whole Veggie-Stuffed Trout	40
Whole-Grain Dutch Baby Pancake	30
Whole-grain Pancakes	28
Wholesome Broccoli Pork Chops	53
Wild Rice Salad with Cranberries and Almonds	84
Winter Chicken and Citrus Salad	83
Wonderful Steamed Artichoke	71

Z

Zucchini Salad with Ranch Dip	80
Zucchini Soup with Roasted Chickpeas	87

Made in the USA
Monee, IL
22 August 2021